Europe and Northern Ireland's Future

Comparative Political Economy
Series Editor: Erik Jones

A major new series exploring contemporary issues in comparative political economy. Pluralistic in approach, the books offer original, theoretically informed analyses of the interaction between politics and economics, and explore the implications for policy at the regional, national and supranational level.

Published

Europe and Northern Ireland's Future
Mary C. Murphy

The New Politics of Trade
Alasdair R. Young

Europe and Northern Ireland's Future

Negotiating Brexit's Unique Case

Mary C. Murphy

agenda
publishing

For Paul

First published in 2018 by Agenda Publishing

Agenda Publishing Limited
The Core
Science Central
Bath Lane
Newcastle upon Tyne
NE4 5TF
www.agendapub.com

ISBN 978-1-78821-029-4 (hardcover)
ISBN 978-1-78821-030-0 (paperback)

British Library Cataloguing-in-Publication Data
A catalogue record for this book is available from the British Library

Typeset by Swales & Willis, Exeter, Devon, UK
Printed and bound in the UK by TJ International

Contents

Acknowledgements

My academic career started with a PhD thesis that documented and analysed Northern Ireland's relationship with the European Union. The choice by the UK to leave the European Union marks the final stage of that relationship in its current form. This book was motivated by the EU referendum decision, and inspired by a belief that despite considerable challenges and given certain conditions, this momentous decision can strengthen rather than undermine Northern Ireland's post-conflict journey.

The research that informs the content of this book was gathered in a number of ways: on a one-to-one basis, at workshops and conferences, and during Chatham House events. Contributions from civil servants, politicians, journalists and stakeholders were hugely important and valuable. Their input and insights helped to enhance the depth and quality of this study. I hope that the final published product repays them with some useful ideas and analysis.

Brexit is, of course, a "moving target". While proposals and agreements will be mooted and proposed over the course of the months and years to come, their feasibility and their acceptance or rejection will be determined by the issues covered in this book. The European Commission's Draft Withdrawal Agreement published in February 2018 is not addressed here, and there will be further documents and developments which will either advance or damage the prospects for an orderly Brexit. This book anticipates these developments and provides a frame of reference within which they can be best understood and assessed.

My thanks to academic colleagues in University College Cork and elsewhere who shared their thoughts and assessments with me. Their input was invaluable and has lent greater rigour to the work. Engagement with academic friends also helped to make the research process enjoyable! The students I have met and taught over the years also (inadvertently) contributed to framing my research. Friends in Cork were hugely supportive too.

I am immensely grateful to the team at Agenda Publishing, particularly Alison Howson, for her extraordinary patience and support. There is no better gift than a dedicated and enthusiastic editor and Alison offered this and more. I am also thankful to the anonymous reviewer and series editors who provided helpful and constructive feedback and advice.

A word of thanks to my parents and family for their permanent support and unrelenting interest in my work. A particular mention for my brother Declan who is always an inspiration. A final thank you to my best friend, my husband Paul. He knows more about Brexit than he may ever need or wish to know! Through it all, his love and support has been unfailing.

Mary C. Murphy
Cork

Foreword

Erik Jones

The lesson that we learned from Britain's 2016 referendum on the European Union is that European integration is experienced differently in different places. This is obviously true across countries, and always has been the case. The British referendum revealed the extent to which such distinctiveness is also true within member states. The British vote was surprising because of the concentration of support for membership in the European Union in places like London, Oxford and Cambridge. It was also surprising for the concentration of desire to leave the European Union in many parts of Britain outside of those major cities. There were of course important exceptions. Scotland and Northern Ireland were most prominent among these. And, in the immediate aftermath of the vote, there was considerable concern that Scots might take advantage of the difference in attitudes to push for another referendum on independence. That seemed to be the most potent source of division within the United Kingdom.

What few observers recognized at the outset, however, were the full implications of the Northern Irish case. To say that Northern Ireland's relationship with European integration is "distinctive" is an understatement. The Northern Irish peace process was framed by European Union membership both for Ireland and for the United Kingdom. In the two decades that followed the Good Friday Agreement, the people of Northern Ireland grew accustomed to being able to interact freely both with the British and with the Irish economy thanks to this European Union membership.

The decision of the British people to leave the European Union threatened much of this new freedom. In doing so, and inadvertently, that decision also threatened the post-conflict stabilization of Northern

Ireland. This potential disruption was difficult to appreciate for any but the closest observers of Northern Irish politics. Even within the British government, the distinctive position of Northern Ireland relative to European Union membership was under-explored. This became all the more true in the aftermath of the May 2017 British general election. When the Conservative Party chose to form a minority government with the support of the Northern Irish Democratic Unionist Party, it inadvertently raised the prospect that the interests of one group within Northern Ireland might be privileged by this new government, perhaps even over the stability of the Northern Irish peace process.

This prospect of weakening the implementation of the Good Friday Agreement became particularly important in the negotiation of trade relations and regulatory convergence between the British economy and the European Union. At issue was the necessity for having a hard border between Northern Ireland and the rest of Ireland as a result of Britain's desire to exit from the single internal market of the European Union. The reason this might be so is something that we explored already in this series in the book *The New Politics of Trade*, by Alasdair Young. The new politics of global trade takes place deep beyond national borders; if that politics is rejected, then only strong national borders can provide the kind of safeguards necessary to ensure that goods passing from one market to the next meet the essential regulatory requirements. Hence even if no one declares a goal of introducing a hard border between Northern Ireland and the rest of the island – or, indeed, between Northern Ireland and the rest of the UK – such a border might be a necessary consequence of how the negotiations between Great Britain and the European Union play out.

There is no simple way to understand the complexity of politics and economics involved in this dispute over whether and to what extent Britain's decision to leave the European Union will result in the introduction of border controls for Northern Ireland. There is also no simple way to anticipate the social consequences of whatever outcome may result from Britain's negotiations with the European Union. European integration is perceived differently in different parts of Europe and has different implications for different groups of Europeans. Moreover, those nuances at play can be quite important. They may even make the difference between peace and conflict. Whether that will be the case of

Northern Ireland requires more background and understanding than most analysts deploy. A special guide is needed.

Mary C. Murphy provides just that kind of insight. Her book, *Europe and Northern Ireland's Future* is a tight and detailed introduction to the unique circumstances that make up the multidimensional relationship between Northern Ireland, the United Kingdom, Ireland and the rest of the European Union. The great strength of Murphy's analysis is the long historical sweep she's able to cover. Murphy has followed Northern Ireland's relationship with the European Union for many years. She has a deep familiarity with the Northern Irish peace process and its social implications on both sides, Catholic and Protestant. And she is able to bring all of that insight to bear on current debates. Her analysis shows the strength of political economy in bringing together both the theory of market practice and the reality of market institutions and their accompanying political and social arrangements. We are very grateful to Mary for agreeing to share her understanding of the Northern Irish situation. We believe anyone who reads this book will come away with a better grasp of where Northern Ireland is today and how it is likely to evolve whatever the outcome of negotiations over Britain's exit from European Union membership. We hope you will agree.

Abbreviations

APNI	Alliance Party of Northern Ireland
BIC	British–Irish Council
CAP	Common Agricultural Policy
CBI	Confederation of British Industry
CTA	Common Travel Area
DUP	Democratic Unionist Party
EAFRD	European Agricultural Fund for Rural Development
EEA	European Economic Area
EEC	European Economic Community
EP	European Parliament
ERDF	European Regional Development Fund
ESF	European Social Fund
ESRI	Economic and Social Research Institute
FDI	Foreign Direct Investment
GVA	Gross Value Added
JHA	Justice and Home Affairs
MLA	Member of the Legislative Assembly
NISRA	Northern Ireland Statistics and Research Agency
NITF	Northern Ireland–EU Taskforce
NSMC	North/South Ministerial Council
ONIEB	Office of the Northern Ireland Executive in Brussels
PBPA	People Before Profit Alliance
RHI	Renewable Heat Incentive
SDLP	Social Democratic and Labour Party
SEM	Single European Market
SFP	Single Farm Payment
SNP	Scottish National Party
TD	Teachta Dála (the Gaelic term for Member of Parliament)
UFU	Ulster Farmers' Union

UKIP   United Kingdom Independence Party
UUP   Ulster Unionist Party
WTO   World Trade Organization

1

The political economy of a pressured relationship

After a prolonged period of conflict spanning four decades, political violence in Northern Ireland has dissipated. Agreement on the creation of power-sharing institutions was achieved in 1998 and has been followed by a lowering of tensions between the nationalist and unionist communities. Relations between Northern Ireland and the Republic of Ireland, and between the UK and Ireland have simultaneously been transformed.[1] Economic growth and prosperity has materialized on both sides of the border. All of these positive developments have happened against the backdrop of joint Irish and UK membership of the European Union (EU).

The June 2016 referendum decision to exit the EU represents a critical moment for the UK, and for its constituent parts. The outcome and aftermath of the vote revealed the existence of marked political, ideological, socio-economic, demographic and geographic divisions across the UK. The Northern Ireland electorate voted for the UK to remain in the EU. Of those who voted in Northern Ireland, 55.8 per cent supported the UK's continued membership. This result is at odds with the overall UK referendum result, which narrowly supported the Leave position. Like Scotland, London and Gibraltar, the Northern Ireland preference for Remain was subsumed by the UK-wide preference for Leave. The suspension of Northern Ireland's devolved institutions in early 2017 followed in May by elections to the Northern Ireland Assembly and then shortly after that a UK general election

---

1. The island of Ireland contains two jurisdictions: Northern Ireland, which is part of the United Kingdom, and the Republic of Ireland. For the purposes of clarity, these terms will be used throughout. References to the island of Ireland relate to the entire island and the two jurisdictions.

added an intriguingly unexpected dimension to the question of how to deal with Northern Ireland interests during and after UK withdrawal. A loose political pact between the Conservative Party and Northern Ireland's Eurosceptic Democratic Unionist Party (DUP) prompted very real concerns about the impact of such a move on the shape of the UK's Brexit deal and on what the new UK government arithmetic might mean for political stability in Northern Ireland.

Given Northern Ireland's geographic situation, its close economic and institutional ties with the Republic of Ireland, its political history of conflict, and the existence of a communal divide on the question of EU membership, the implications of the overall Leave vote were more profound for Northern Ireland than for any other part of the UK. The referendum result effectively meant that Northern Ireland was politically and economically vulnerable, and more concerning was that the region had no champion in terms of defending and advancing its specific interests. Neither the Northern Ireland Executive nor the local political parties were able to forge a common position on Brexit and the UK government paid only limited attention to the implications of EU withdrawal for the region. In contrast, the Irish government was much more vocal and proactive in highlighting issues for both sides of the border. The EU also afforded consideration to specific Irish and Northern Ireland interests. Overall however, the Northern Ireland situation was largely a footnote in the broader national Brexit referendum debate. This was not just regrettable, but reckless. The political and economic forces to which Northern Ireland is subject were profoundly challenged by Brexit, and produced some economic and political turbulence. Long-term this may involve severe political implications for the region itself, and also entail serious consequences for the UK and the Republic of Ireland. The fracturing of relationships in Northern Ireland, on the island of Ireland and between the Republic of Ireland and the UK, potentially threatens political and constitutional stability. The EU referendum vote added an additional layer of (tense) complexity to the troubled Northern Ireland polity, which risks igniting broader economic and political turmoil for the neighbouring states. The Republic of Ireland's continued membership of the EU means that the Union is implicated here too.

Northern Ireland has been a region in transition since the 1990s. The calling of paramilitary ceasefires in 1994 and the signing of the

Belfast Agreement less than four years later jumpstarted a period of regional economic revival and political stability. The region also weathered the global economic crisis and managed to maintain peace and stability despite sporadic political crises. The 2016 *Northern Ireland Peace Monitoring Report* (Wilson 2016) depicted a region in transition – one that faces continuing economic, political, security and social challenges, but that has nevertheless experienced some success in the bedding down of devolved institutions and in advancing community relations. The process of reconciliation and community integration is slow however, and the challenges that persist are complex and multifaceted. What Galtung (1990) labels a "negative peace" prevails in Northern Ireland. This environment is characterized by lingering disagreements and tensions that contribute to the ongoing polarization of the two communities. Even after the ceasefires and the signing of the 1998 Belfast Agreement, Northern Ireland occupied a volatile political context. The Irish language, legacy issues, flags and symbols continue to be a thorn in the side of an incomplete peace process, the final stages of which are always the most vexing. Northern Ireland also retains an "essential 'inbetweenness' of a political space that has moved from a 'long war' through a 'long peace' and into a profoundly undecided future" (Shirlow & Coulter 2014: 713). The process of conflict management and resolution is long-term and imperfect. Given the tenuous nature of the local settlement, future peace, prosperity and stability may be derailed by unexpected and unanticipated forces. Brexit has the potential to be one such force.

On the cusp of remarkable changes – not of its own making or choice – Northern Ireland may simultaneously be collateral damage, and the cause of further collateral damage. Brexit has challenged the current status quo in Northern Ireland and disrupted the region's economic and political trajectory. This book delivers a strong cautionary message about the imprudence of overlooking the needs, interests, preferences and aspirations of the UK's most troubled region at a moment of extraordinary constitutional change. It provides a detailed and in-depth overview and analysis of key economic and political factors for Northern Ireland. It analyses the potential impact of Brexit on Northern Ireland, and details how what happens in Northern Ireland may have substantial and far-reaching political, economic and constitutional effects for the UK and the Republic of Ireland.

Devolution and the UK

Northern Ireland's EU relationship can only be understood within the broader UK national context. Since joining the European Economic Community (EEC) in 1973, the UK's political system changed through the devolution process. The devolution of powers to Scotland, Wales and Northern Ireland was initiated and implemented by former Prime Minister Tony Blair in the late 1990s. This process of regionalization was in line with a broader trend towards the embrace of various forms of decentralization in many European states. A range of factors including globalization, nationalism, and EU developments influenced "a general renaissance of the regional level" (Bullman 1997: 4) and the UK was not removed from this trend. Northern Ireland's devolved institutions grew out of this environment, although importantly their consociational, power-sharing arrangement was primarily rooted in attempts at conflict resolution.

Northern Ireland and devolution: The 1998 Belfast Agreement

The Belfast Agreement is a historic compromise agreed by the majority of Northern Ireland's political parties on Good Friday, 10 April 1998. At the heart of the Agreement lies the principle of consent, which affirms that there will be no change to Northern Ireland's constitutional status as a part of the UK unless a majority of the people of Ireland, north and south, vote for change. This central provision of the Agreement effectively legitimized the nationalist aspiration for a united Ireland, and simultaneously provided guarantees for unionists by confirming that there was currently no majority support for a united Ireland. The Agreement also put in place an institutional framework that aimed to manage relationships within Northern Ireland, between Northern Ireland and the Republic of Ireland, and between the two islands. The framework comprises three separate but interlocking institutional strands: the Northern Ireland Assembly, the North/South Ministerial Council (NSMC) and the British–Irish Council (BIC) (see Table 1.1). The Agreement also addresses other facets of the conflict and contains provisions in relation to human rights, equality, the decommissioning of weapons, the early release of paramilitary prisoners, security and policing.

Table 1.1 The Belfast Agreement (1998): key strands

Strand	Characteristic	Institutions
Strand 1	Internal	A directly elected 108-member Northern Ireland Assembly operating on a cross-community basis with full legislative and executive control over "transferred matters" (and some reserved matters).*
Strand 2	North–South	The North/South Ministerial Council (NSMC) comprises representatives from the Irish government and the devolved Northern Ireland administration. It meets in sectoral and plenary format "to develop consultation, co-operation and action within the island of Ireland – including through implementation on an all-island and cross-border basis – on matters of mutual interest within the competence of the Administrations, North and South" (Strand 2, Paragraph 1).**
Strand 3	East–West	The British–Irish Council comprises representatives from the UK and Irish governments; representatives of the devolved administrations in Scotland, Northern Ireland and Wales; and representatives from the Isle of Man and Channel Islands. The Council was established "to promote the harmonious and mutually beneficial development of the totality of relationships among the peoples of these islands" (Strand 3, Paragraph 1). It aims to reach agreement on cooperation on matters of mutual interest and does so through discussion, consultation and the exchange of information.***

* The size of the Northern Ireland Assembly has since been reduced to 90 members.
** The Belfast Agreement stipulates a range of areas for North–South cooperation and implementation: agriculture; education; transport; environment; waterways; social security/social welfare; relevant EU programmes; inland fisheries; aquaculture and marine matters; health; and urban and rural development. The work of the NSMC is supported by a series of all-island implementation bodies: one such body is the Special EU Programmes Body (SEUPB), which oversees cross-border EU funding programmes.
*** The Belfast Agreement is less prescriptive in relation to areas of BIC cooperation, when compared to the NSMC. However, the Agreement does suggest that suitable areas for early discussion may include transport links, agricultural issues, environmental issues, cultural issues, health issues, education issues and approaches to EU issues. The work of the BIC has since expanded to 12 work-streams.

The Northern Ireland Assembly, which is overseen by the Executive, facilitates power-sharing. The single transferable vote (PR-STV) electoral system used to elect Members of the Legislative Assembly (MLAs) allocates seats in relative proportion to votes won. The Assembly also conducts its business using specific legislative voting mechanisms designed to achieve cross-community support,[2] and the ministerial appointment procedure is based on the d'Hondt system,[3] which also effectively guarantees representation for both communities.

The Northern Ireland Assembly enjoys full executive and legislative control over "transferred" matters. These are primarily in the economic and social field.[4] The Assembly may also legislate in respect of "reserved" matters subject to various consents, but has not yet done so to any significant degree.[5] "Excepted" matters remain the responsibility of Westminster and the UK central government. The Northern Ireland Assembly does not have competence to legislate in these areas.[6]

---

2. Key decisions must have cross-community support. This is achieved by using one of two voting methods. The use of parallel consent requires a majority of those members present and voting, including a majority of the unionist and nationalist designations present and voting. The weighted majority method requires that at least 60 per cent of members are present and voting, including at least 40 per cent of each of the nationalist and unionist designations present and voting.

3. The First Minister and Deputy First Minister are jointly elected by the Assembly voting on a cross-community basis. Other members of the Northern Ireland Executive are allocated to parties on the basis of the d'Hondt system by reference to the number of seats each party has in the Assembly. Prior to the suspension of the Northern Ireland Assembly in early 2017, there were ten members of the Northern Ireland Executive (including the First Minister and Deputy First Minister). The DUP had five portfolios and Sinn Féin had four. Due to the contentious nature of the Justice portfolio, the Minister of Justice is appointed by a cross-community Assembly vote and not by the d'Hondt system. The most recent Minister of Justice was Independent MLA, Claire Sugden. The SDLP and UUP chose not to participate in the Northern Ireland Executive following the 2016 Assembly election. Instead both parties opted to take the role of official Opposition; the first time since 1998 that the Northern Ireland Assembly had an official Opposition.

4. The Northern Ireland Assembly has full legislative powers in the following areas: health and social services; education; employment and skills; agriculture; social security; pensions and child support; housing; economic development; local government; environmental issues, including planning; transport; culture and sport; the Northern Ireland Civil Service; equal opportunities; and justice and policing.

5. Reserved matters include, among others: import and export controls; international trade and financial markets; disqualification from Assembly membership; and intellectual property.

6. Excepted matters include: the constitution; Royal succession; international relations; defence and armed forces; nationality, immigration and asylum; elections; national security; nuclear energy; UK-wide taxation; currency; conferring of honours; and international treaties.

The Belfast Agreement and the institutions it creates have been an important means of preserving relative peace in Northern Ireland. Despite sporadic suspensions of the power-sharing institutions, the Agreement has facilitated the peaceful expression of difference within an institutional setting acceptable to both communities. The conflict is managed, although not necessarily fully resolved, within this unique political landscape.

Altered relationships: The UK, the EU and devolution

The UK process of asymmetrical devolution from the late 1990s included arrangements specific to the different regions, but importantly, it did not definitively settle constitutional agitation. Indeed, the UK's constitutional past, present and future continue to be a live issue. The Scottish referendum result against independence in 2014 failed to fully assuage questions relating to Scottish independence. During the EU referendum campaign, Scottish independence was a central issue and at the forefront of political discourse. The 2017 general election result, however, was not a good one for the Scottish National Party (SNP) and talk of a second independence referendum subsided. The possibility of UK constitutional change was also aired during and after the referendum in Northern Ireland. Sinn Féin equated the Northern Ireland Remain result, and the party's increased electoral strength, with support for a united Ireland. The Conservative Party post-election alliance with the DUP in June 2017 also pushed the issue of Irish unity back on to the table as nationalists railed against a British government tied to unionism.

As the UK's constitution has changed, so too has the country's relationship with the EU, which has become increasingly troubled and more complex. This was evident within established political parties, particularly the Conservative Party, which has long been riven with intense division over the European question. The actions of former Conservative Party leader David Cameron were instrumental in setting the scene for the UK decision to leave the EU in June 2016. Facing a clear electoral challenge from the small, but ardently anti-EU UK Independence Party (UKIP), David Cameron committed to hold a referendum on UK membership of the EU should the Conservative

Party be returned to power following the 2015 general election. The former prime minister's decision to offer a plebiscite was ostensibly about improving the appeal of the Conservative Party at the ballot box and confronting the electoral threat posed by UKIP. It also aimed to placate the increasingly vocal anti-EU wing of the Tory Party. It is clear that Cameron's decision to promise a referendum on EU member-ship was motivated by "domestic party political and electoral reasons" (Hobolt 2016: 1261; see also Glencross 2016: 9–10). The Tories were not expected to win the 2015 Westminster election. A hung parliament was widely anticipated, and this would have meant no referendum on EU membership. However, in a surprise result, the electoral contest returned a Conservative Party victory and the EU referendum would follow just over a year later. The strongly pro-EU Liberal Democrats were the main casualties of the 2015 general election. Having served in a coalition government with the larger Conservative Party from 2010, the Liberal Democrats were sorely punished by voters in 2015. Their representation in Westminster went from 57 to just eight MPs. The collapse in support for the party was not necessarily a rejection by the voting public of Liberal Democrat support for the EU, but it did mean that the strength of Europhile voices was diminished. The depth of the Labour Party's support for Europe was also challenged following the 2015 general election when the commitment of the party to the EU showed signs of wavering. Jeremy Corbyn replaced Ed Miliband as leader of the party. Corbyn was known for being notoriously anti-EU. In the 1975 UK referendum on EU membership, he voted against the UK remaining in the EU. He was later opposed to the Maastricht Treaty and voted against the Lisbon Treaty during a House of Commons vote. He has a record of being highly critical of the EU. However, despite his anti-EU stances, the Labour Party under Corbyn campaigned for the UK to remain in the EU during the 2016 referendum. Corbyn's previous Eurosceptic rhetoric, however, undermined the depth of his Remain message and Leave campaigners ridiculed his supposed new-found enthusiasm for the EU.

The UK's political parties have both shaped British public attitudes to the EU, and reacted to heightened Eurosceptic sentiment among voters. Increasing political and public opposition to the EU has been influenced by a series of historic and contemporary factors. The UK's late accession to the EU in 1973 (16 years after the creation of the EEC) was reflective of a certain ambivalence towards the EU, which has been recalibrated in the intervening period: "The relationship between nationalism and internationalism has been cast in very different terms from those that gave rise to UK membership of the Common Market" (Armstrong 2017: 19). The notion of "taking back control", a desire to reassert British sovereignty, fears around migration and concerns about the cost of EU membership collectively led to increased support for Eurosceptic forces in British politics, and ultimately resulted in the UK vote to leave the EU.

Political and constitutional developments have happened in tandem with the evolution of the Northern Ireland–EU relationship. To some extent, devolution empowered the UK's regions *vis-à-vis* the EU as they were granted some responsibility for the implementation of EU policies. Simultaneously however, discussion of the UK's place in Europe was becoming an increasingly contested issue at the national level. The bulk of this contestation was emanating from England, and was influential in terms of forcing a debate and ultimately a referendum (see Henderson *et al.* 2017). This scenario was materializing just as Northern Ireland was contemplating the difficult final stages and (possibly) endpoint of the conflict. The 2016 EU referendum marked a return to older and unsettling arguments about the practical operation, political status and symbolic meaning of the border between Northern Ireland and the Republic of Ireland.

A "pressured" relationship: Northern Ireland and the EU

Northern Ireland's relationship with the EU has traditionally been low-key and largely uncontroversial. Unlike other parts of the UK, attitudes to the EU are less hostile in Northern Ireland. In fact, Northern Ireland has tended to be among the more Europhile of UK regions. The approach to EU matters has been based on a typically pragmatic form of engagement rooted in economic self-interest (see Murphy 2014).

The Northern Ireland–EU relationship has differed from that of other European and UK regions by virtue of the Troubles that plagued the region from the late 1960s to the mid-1990s. The UK joined the EU just as the Northern Ireland conflict was reaching its most intense period and in the period since 1973, the conflict and its legacy have been the backdrop against which that relationship has played out. In that context, it is possible to identify different phases in the relationship between this politically troubled and economically challenged region and the EU.

1973–88: Distracted and detached

The first 15 years of UK membership were marked by small doses of enthusiasm in Northern Ireland for the EEC, but otherwise dominated by patterns of detachment. Membership coincided with the introduction of Direct Rule of the region by Westminster and the intensification of sectarian violence. The relentlessness and awfulness of the Troubles disproportionately occupied the minds of politicians and public alike. Discussions concerning the EU's supposed potential to challenge this environment were little in evidence. The view that the EU may empower the Northern Ireland region (economically and/or politically) was not appreciated. Sovereignty and national identity were the filters through which political positions on Europe were articulated. The nationalist SDLP was very much in favour of EU membership whereas unionists and republicans objected to its impact on British sovereignty and Irish sovereignty respectively. More broadly, Guelke (1988: 155) has noted that "there was a relatively muted reaction in the province to actual entry to the Community". During this period, the EU was a peripheral political issue in Northern Ireland.

The persistent focus of Northern Ireland's relationship with the EU throughout the period of Direct Rule remained resolutely fixed on economic considerations. Financial support from the EEC's structural funds and Community Initiatives were welcomed, as was support for the agricultural and fisheries policies. Northern Ireland was also categorized as a priority region for EU structural fund assistance (see Trimble 1990). The region "received 9.6 per cent of the UK's ERDF [European Regional Development Fund] funds in the period 1973–1987 and 17.0 per cent of its ESF [European Social Fund] funding" (Gudgin 2000: 46). The economic and financial impact of EU membership was the primary means via which the potential benefits of membership were appreciated in Northern Ireland. This did not, however, prevent some actors from suggesting that EU membership might impact positively on a possible resolution of the conflict. Hayward and Murphy (2012) note that this period saw some subtle developments that spoke to ideas about how the EU might impact on the Northern Ireland conflict. Leader of the nationalist SDLP frequently referenced how Northern Ireland should use the EU as an example or model of conflict resolution. The EU facilitated bilateral discussions between the UK and Irish governments in their search for peace during this decade and a half. The European Parliament (EP) produced an interesting analysis of the Northern Ireland conflict. The Haagerup Report (1984) was drawn up by the EP's Political Affairs Committee and named after its rapporteur, the Danish MEP Niels Haagerup. Following the signing of the Anglo–Irish Agreement in 1985, the EU also publically pledged both economic and political support. These events aside however, the EU was of minor significance for politicians and for the public in Northern Ireland. Other more pressing security and constitutional concerns were prioritized, and the EU was side-lined as a result.

1989–2006: Economically engaged

From the late 1980s, Northern Ireland's relationship with the EU began to shift. The drive to complete the Single European Market (SEM) by 1992 altered Europe's business environment and led to greater opportunities, but also stiffer competition. The uneven ability of peripheral and disadvantaged regions in particular to meet the challenges of the SEM led to the doubling of EU structural funding to assist those regions and to help offset the negative effects of increased market pressures in the new and open European economic arena. This reform of the structural funds increased Northern Ireland receipts from the funds because the region was classified as having "Objective 1" status. This classification was applied to EU regions where GDP per capita was less than 75 per cent of the EU average. Although Northern Ireland's GDP per capita was above this ceiling throughout the period, the region nevertheless qualified for this assistance on the basis of the so-called "special circumstances" pertaining to the region. This was a reference to the impact of the conflict on Northern Ireland's socio-economic position.

The precise impact of the SEM on Northern Ireland's economic development is unclear: "Northern Ireland's standing, as regards regional disparities, has not improved since entry, but how much this is due to membership is debatable" (Hainsworth 1996: 136). The Troubles raged on during the early 1990s and arguably prevented Northern Ireland from capitalizing on the opportunities available through the SEM. Inward investment and local economic development were victims of an unstable political and social environment. An important feature of the drive to complete the SEM was the gradual removal of the economic border between Northern Ireland and the Republic of Ireland. Membership of the SEM meant that the physical infrastructure of border controls and customs posts was no longer necessary. The process of dismantling physical and technical barriers to trade was economically advantageous but importantly, it was also politically welcome, particularly for nationalists. The physical manifestation of a border on the island of Ireland highlighted its division and undermined nationalist identification with the rest of Ireland. The end of economic borders was soon accompanied by the removal of security checkpoints in the context of the achievement of peace and a political settlement. By the end of this period, the only signs of a physical border were a change in road signage.

The search for a resolution to the Northern Ireland conflict, which had been ongoing since the end of the 1980s, culminated in the paramilitary ceasefires of 1994 and the signing of the Belfast Agreement four years later in 1998. The EU reacted to developments in Northern Ireland by committing financial aid to the region. The Peace programme (now in its fourth iteration) was created in 1995 and was constructed to complement and support peace-building efforts. In addition, the Peace programmes can be regarded as "specifically designed conflict transformation tool[s]" (Buchanan 2008: 387). The programmes are unusual in how they facilitate the management of EU financial aid and the process of allocation in Northern Ireland. All Peace programmes involve support for bottom-up actions rooted in local and regional partnership arrangements, and based on the close and heavy involvement of civil society. The programmes have largely focused on addressing specific problems, of an economic and social nature, which are linked to the legacy of the conflict. In this way, the programmes have financed a range of measures including economic regeneration, social inclusion and reconciliation, and they have relied on the use of partnership approaches that are uniquely tailored to foster and encourage cross-community cooperation. Following the creation of cross-border implementation bodies, some of the Peace funds are channelled through the Special EU Programmes Body (SEUPB), created under the terms of the 1998 Belfast Agreement and overseen by the NSMC.

The devolution of powers to Northern Ireland also occurred during this period. The stability of the new power-sharing administration was tested during the early years when a number of suspensions interrupted the roll-out of devolved power. The persistence of political difficulties and the need to adapt to a new political reality presented politicians and administrators with challenges. The terms of the devolution settlement required newly created institutions to engage with the EU dimension to Northern Ireland public policy responsibilities. This was slow to materialize, and initially it focused heavily on establishing a Northern Ireland presence in Brussels. The Office of the Northern Ireland Executive (ONIEB) opened in Brussels in 2001. A number of other developments are noteworthy including the work of what was the European Policy Coordination Unit (EPCU) in the Executive Office and the Northern Ireland Assembly's Committee of the Centre, which in 2002 conducted a European Inquiry and produced a Report. The latter included prescriptions for the development of a Northern Ireland–EU strategy. Murphy (2007: 311) notes that during this period there were: "subtle degrees of institutional adaptation, the gradual evolution of formal and informal linkages and changes to the process of policy making and decision making".

During the period after 1988, the EU certainly became a more economically important force in Northern Ireland. Given the moves towards peace, the EU itself was able to realize a financially supportive role in Northern Ireland. Key protagonists were receptive and EU support did not offend the British government. The EU's role was largely rooted in an approach that linked economic support and peacebuilding. The financial commitment was welcomed and seized. The political dimension to engagement with the EU was evident, but it was subtle, and it did not extend to deeper public engagement. Northern Ireland citizens demonstrated a utilitarian as opposed to an affective interest in the EU (see McGowan & O'Connor 2004). They viewed EU membership as having provided material benefits including improved human rights, access to the single market, better working conditions, environmental advances and a greater say for the UK in trade negotiations (see European Commission 2007).

2007–14: Dynamism and discord

The Northern Ireland–EU relationship entered a new era following the re-establishment of devolved institutions in 2007 after a protracted five-year period of suspension. The period is marked by two contradictory themes – dynamism and discord. The dynamism is evident in terms of increased engagement between the Northern Ireland devolved administration and the EU authorities in Brussels. The discord relates to the negative impact of the global economic crisis on Northern Ireland, on EU fortunes and on local attitudes to the EU. It also alludes to enduring political differences in Northern Ireland that demonstrated a European slant prior to the EU referendum.

A positive development following the resurrection of the Northern Ireland devolved institutions in May 2007 was the European Commission-sponsored creation of the Northern Ireland–EU Taskforce (NITF), which established a strategic partnership between Northern Ireland and the Brussels-based institution. The initiative was an express attempt, on the part of the Commission, to support and help consolidate the return to devolved power in Northern Ireland (Hayward & Murphy 2012). By strategically connecting Northern Ireland interests and Commission officials, the NITF facilitated improved engagement with the EU by prompting agreement on a series of Northern Ireland–EU actions, strategies and forward-planning exercises. During this period too, the scope of Northern Ireland's external relations expanded, particularly with respect to the Republic of Ireland. On EU issues, there existed a culture of information sharing, regular political contact and the emergence of shared all-island positions between the two jurisdictions (Murphy 2011: 562): "Since May 2007 in particular (when devolved power was returned to Northern Ireland), relations between the ONIEB and the Irish Permanent Representation (Perm Rep) have developed in interesting ways."

Northern Ireland also continued to benefit from EU largesse in the form of the structural funds and the Peace programme. For all the progress after 2007 however, difficulties of a political nature persisted. Tense relations between the parties to the Northern Ireland Executive did not always allow for positive responsiveness to the EU. On occasion, local political tensions challenged Northern Ireland's progressively more pragmatic approach to engagement with the EU. Agreement on the construction of an EU-sponsored Centre for Conflict Resolution was seriously delayed and eventually shelved due to political differences between Sinn Féin and the DUP during this period (see Hayward & Murphy 2012).

After 2015: Influence and intrigue

The period from 2015 was punctured by two UK general elections, two Assembly elections, political scandal in Northern Ireland, party leadership changes and the UK referendum on EU membership of the EU. The promise by the former UK Prime Minister David Cameron to hold a referendum on the UK's membership of the EU kick-started a debate on the merits and otherwise of the UK's relationship with the EU. The referendum was preceded by the 2016 Northern Ireland Assembly election, which largely left the political balance and electoral status quo intact in Northern Ireland. The referendum campaign itself was ill-tempered, divisive and sometimes misleading. From the early days, however, there was an expectation that the vote Remain camp would win the plebiscite, and probably do so decisively. The referendum result, however, delivered a very unexpected outcome. By a slim margin of 51.9 per cent, the UK voted to leave the EU. In contrast to the UK as a whole, however, Northern Ireland returned a 55.8 per cent majority vote to remain.

The Northern Ireland result was in fact lower than had been anticipated by pollsters, and so too was the turnout figure. The breakdown of the result demonstrates, however, that the profile of voters who supported Remain was similar to other parts of the UK (Garry 2016: 6):

> In short there does seem to be evidence supporting the idea that there is a cluster of traits (low education and skill) and beliefs (anti-immigrant, socially conservative, alienated from politics) associated with the leave vote in Northern Ireland that is consistent with the "left behind by liberal globalization" argument elaborated in the rest of the UK.

There was also a political dimension to the Northern Ireland referendum result. In terms of party political preferences, Northern Ireland voters largely followed the cues provided by their traditional political

15

party allegiances. DUP voters were strongly in favour of Leave while nationalist voters were strongly in favour of Remain.

The referendum campaign in Northern Ireland was less spirited and less testy than for the rest of the UK. Slow to develop and lacking in energy and dynamism, the debate was muted. The referendum outcome also appears to have not engaged Northern Ireland's political parties. Despite the serious questions and challenges posed by Brexit for Northern Ireland, the devolved administration was unable to agree a position on how the region should approach the issue. Other more localized political issues exercised the minds of Northern Ireland's political class, including residual conflict issues. Two more trips to the polls followed and both produced intriguing results – a strong Sinn Féin surge, an uneven DUP electoral performance, and the holding of the middle ground. The ten Westminster seats won by the DUP in 2017 are particularly noteworthy. When combined with the reduced seat tally for the Conservative Party, the small unionist party effectively held the balance of power. The DUP's decision to sign a confidence-and-supply agreement with the Tories provided some leverage over the new government's programme and an enviable position at the heart of UK political decision-making – a development that prompted anger and concern among nationalists. The continued suspension of power-sharing institutions in Northern Ireland minimized the opportunities for a broader and less partisan Northern Ireland voice to emerge, and prevented the Northern Ireland Executive from contributing to the Brexit discussion at the UK centre.

The EU emerged as an issue of serious contestation for the UK during the period after 2015. The UK's referendum decision exposed marked differences in preference between the constituent parts of the UK. For Northern Ireland, the referendum decision complicated the challenges already being faced by the devolved power-sharing system.

Conclusion

Northern Ireland's early experience of the EU can be characterized as distant and detached. A violent conflict and more pressing political concerns closer to home prevented any sort of deep engagement with the EU and EU issues. As the European integration process advanced from the 1980s, Northern Ireland participated in the SEM and enjoyed access to structural funding. The evolving peace process, the signing of the 1998 Belfast Agreement, the rolling out of devolved power-sharing arrangements; all were subtly supported by practical and financial EU support. This lent greater visibility to the EU in Northern Ireland although it did not mean a convergence of EU perspectives and positions among Northern Ireland's political parties. The tenor of Northern Ireland's relationship with the EU, much of it filtered through the devolved power-sharing institutions and North–South bodies after 1998, permitted a functional and pragmatic engagement with the EU. This approach was largely able to co-exist with differing Northern Ireland political perspectives ranging from Euroscepticism to Europhilia. The EU evoked difference and division, but EU issues were not politicized and rarely had a polarizing effect on the Northern Ireland administration. The referendum, however, brought new EU issues and questions to the fore. These were more political and less functional in character, and they exposed some stark differences between Northern Ireland's political parties and two communities. Having slowly cultivated a pragmatic form of engagement with the EU, the period after 2015 may have fractured an aspect of the operation of Northern Ireland's contemporary political system that had not been seriously infected by age-old rivalries and constitutional battles. Chapter 2 examines how the EU referendum campaign, and related political events and developments, placed challenging and contested political and constitutional questions on the Northern Ireland agenda, and how this contributed to the politicization of what had previously been a mainly neutral and anodyne policy environment where potent political differences were rarely in evidence.

2

The politicization of Brexit in Northern Ireland

In a European context, George (1998) has labelled the UK "an awkward partner". This characterization of the UK's place in Europe is based, to a high degree, on what former Prime Minister Tony Blair described as a history of "hesitation, alienation, incomprehension" (quoted in Watts & Pilkington 2005: 244). The UK chose to opt out of a series of EU policies and developments including the single currency, Schengen, the Charter of Fundamental Rights, and Justice and Home Affairs (JHA) issues. This reflects the unease that EU membership evokes at the national level. UK membership of the EU has long been a contested issue in British politics and has exposed divisions between national political parties, and within those same political parties. The intense divisiveness of the EU issue influenced the creation of a new anti-EU political party, UKIP in 1991. The EU has also sharply divided the national media, interest groups and public opinion in Britain.

Although the two communities in Northern Ireland and their respective political parties have differing perspectives on the merits of European integration, the question of EU membership has not been as contested or as contentious an issue as it has been for the rest of the UK, and for England in particular. The Northern Ireland–EU relationship has a transactional form based on a strong functional character that has included the benefits that come from EU policies and financial assistance. These positive features of Northern Ireland's EU experience have crossed the communal divide. A relatively harmonious relationship has meant that the EU issue in Northern Ireland was never as politicized as it was for other parts of the UK. In a society like Northern Ireland, where individual and group identity is shaped by attachment to political aspirations and related issues, many political, economic, social and cultural issues tend to evoke strong reactions. Where other constitutional questions, and social and economic policies exposed division between the two communities, the EU was not an area of intense political competition or contestation. In 2016, however, the EU referendum unsettled this state of affairs.

Referendums and elections expose societal divisions, and Northern Ireland provides ample evidence of how acrimonious and nasty electoral contests can be. Such moments unleash various political dynamics that can be either positive or negative, and often both. The UK does not have a strong history of direct democracy. There were no referendums before the 1970s. Prior to the 2016 EU referendum, there had been just two national UK referendums – the 1975 referendum on UK membership of the EU (which returned a vote to stay in the EU) and the 2011 referendum on changing the UK electoral system to the alternative vote system (which was rejected). The EU referendum campaign period was pre-dated by the 2015 Westminster election, which placed UK membership of the EU firmly on the national agenda. The surprising Tory victory ensured that the EU theme would continue to animate British politics for many years to come. In Northern Ireland, the 2016 and 2017 Assembly elections, political scandals, changing party leadership and the promised referendum itself meant that Northern Ireland, like the rest of the UK, was offered a multitude of opportunities to consider the EU issue. All of these moments impacted on the positions and behaviours of the two communities, local political parties, leaders and other actors, including the UK government, the Irish government and the EU. Collectively, these forces have contributed to some politicization of the Brexit issue in Northern Ireland. This chapter details how an issue or subject becomes politicized. This is followed by an examination of various political and electoral developments that led to the politicization of the Brexit question in Northern Ireland. The chapter concludes by determining what this shift may mean for the region's future.

The forces of politicization

There is a strong consensus among academic scholars that the EU has been politicized over the past two decades or more (see Zürn 2016). The process of politicization is linked to the decline in the "permissive consensus" or the general support for the EU among the public. This consensus takes the form of passive approval, which tends to be shallowly rooted, but which nevertheless permits government/EU action (see Norris 1997). This type of support for the European integration project, however, was somewhat fragile, and from the 1990s, it is possible to discern a breakdown in the "permissive consensus". Difficulties ratifying the Maastricht Treaty; a sharp drop in public support for the EU; falling turnout at EP elections; and the increasing appeal of Eurosceptic parties highlighted public dissatisfaction with the EU and suggested a crack in the linkage between the citizen and the Union. This period in the EU's recent history, when the permissive consensus began to fracture, is commonly regarded as the moment when the politicization of the EU began. Zürn (2016: 167) posits a useful definition: "Politicization, in general terms, means the demand for, or the act of, transporting an issue or an institution into the field or sphere of politics – making previously unpolitical matters political."

De Wilde *et al.* (2016) identify three components of the concept of politicization that can be observed and/or measured. First, the growing salience of European governance; second, a polarization of opinion; and third, an expansion of actors and audiences engaged in monitoring EU affairs. Ecker-Ehrhardt and Zürn (2013) expand this conception (which tends to rely on the mass media as a source of politicization) and suggest that politicization can also be detected with reference to rising awareness, mobilization and public debates. The forces of politicization can thus be located at three different levels – the micro, meso and macro. At each level, there are three separate means of judging the extent to which politicization occurs. First, the salience of the EU, or an EU issue, can be measured with reference to its relative importance *vis-à-vis* other issues and/or groups, and its coverage by the media. Second, the extent to which the EU, or an EU issue, has a polarizing effect can be determined by examining the beliefs, behaviour and claims of various groups. Third, politicization can be detected if there is an expansion in the number, diversity and mobilization of actors with an interest in the EU or an EU issue. Table 2.1 captures these various dimensions of the politicization phenomena and provides a framework for measuring the extent to which the EU has become politicized.

This examination of Northern Ireland and Brexit uses Zürn's framework to isolate and measure the components and manifestations of

Table 2.1 Components and manifestations of politicization

	Salience	Contestation (polarization)	Expansion of actors
Micro (beliefs)	Importance relative to other issues or institutions	Different beliefs about the issue or the institution	Individuals with different traits (social status, sex, ethnic groups, etc.) see the issue or institution as important
Meso (mobilization)	Importance relative to other targets of mobilization	Mobilized groups stand for different positions	Many different types of group mobilize
Macro (public debates)	Often mentioned in media (relative to other issues)	Polarization of statement/claims	Expansion of contributors to the debate

Source: Zürn (2016: 169).

politicization. An assessment of the changing relative importance of the Brexit issue in Northern Ireland; a determination about the impact of the EU referendum on the mobilization of parties, interest groups and citizens; and an appraisal of the variety and intensity of views that the Brexit debate has provoked, facilitate an overall evaluation of it and how, Brexit has been politicized in Northern Ireland. This analysis is important because politicization can have a polarizing effect. Of course, the consequences of this should not be assumed to be negative or problematic. Different authors have noted different effects. Some link politicization to an increase in support for the EU, while others note the opposite impact (see Hooghe & Marks 2009). In Northern Ireland, however, politicization that polarizes the two communities can invariably be problematic, and in the context of the EU referendum and Brexit, this is where the danger lies. There have been many and varied references to the politicization and the sectarianization of Brexit in Northern Ireland. The DUP's Ian Paisley Jnr (2017) has referred to "politicized arguments" about the issue of the border. SDLP MLA Claire Hanna, speaking at a conference in Dublin in November 2017, talked about the "sectarianization of Brexit" in Northern Ireland. A tweet by UUP MLA Steve Aiken referred to Irish Foreign Affairs Minister Simon Coveney and the Irish government's language being a factor in helping to "sectarianize" Brexit in the eyes of unionists. In a divided society such as Northern Ireland's, politicization is viewed as being inherently negative. Such perceptions, therefore, can be particularly damaging for local politics and community relations in a region that is attempting to leave its troubled past behind.

Northern Ireland is a post-conflict society that continues to work through the final stages of a peace process. Conflict resolution – in its final stages – means not just a de-escalation of violence, but also a change in attitudes and a transformation of relationships at the core of the conflict. In terms of the choreography of a peace process, Northern Ireland is living through a period of relative peace, but minimal rec-onciliation. Violence has stopped, but politics remains polarized – "negative peace" as Galtung (1990) has defined it. In contrast, "positive peace" is defined as the "integration of human society" (Galtung 1964: 2) and involves not just direct peace or an absence of violent conflict, but also structural and cultural peace, which point to the presence of equity and equality, and a culture of peace and dialogue. This form of integration is not wholly evident in Northern Ireland and commenta-tors point to a range of explanations. It is argued that the structure of the power-sharing arrangement in Northern Ireland maintains the community divide.[1] Northern Ireland's distinctive party system is charged with having a similar effect (this is discussed further in the next section). Educational and housing segregation and threats from dissident groups are also impacting negatively on community relations. The 2016 *Peace Monitoring Report* (Wilson 2016) published by the Community Relations Council points to some positive developments in Northern Ireland (although it was published before the suspension of the Assembly in early 2017). Among the negative findings and trends identified are the ongoing scourge of paramilitarism, dissatisfaction with the achievements of the Assembly, the continuing segregation of education and a failure to deal with the past. The politicization of Brexit potentially adds another dimension of polarization to a post-conflict

---

1. An example of this are the cross-community voting mechanisms – parallel con-sent and weighted majority – which require that MLAs designate themselves "unionist", "nationalist" or "other" for the purpose of voting. Critics suggest that this institutionalizes traditional conceptions of identity and so prevents the emer-gence or development of non-communal based parties (see Farry 2009).

society and polity that continues to grapple with division. A politicized public debate on an issue with constitutional connotations risked antagonizing existing political differences between the two communities at a time in the conflict resolution process when the need to build trust and to foster integration is paramount.

The 1994 Northern Ireland paramilitary ceasefires have largely held fast and power-sharing institutions have been operational, albeit on an interrupted basis since 2007. The conflict studies literature notes that these features of a conflict resolution process are but stages along the way to a final sustainable peace, involving a process of conflict transformation, which is deemed "the deepest level of the conflict resolution tradition" (Ramsbotham *et al.* 2011: 9). This level of conflict resolution is synonymous with a process of reconciliation. Speaking to the same theme, but using the label "conflict transformation", Lederach (2014) outlines an expansive process that involves changes in persons, structures and relationships. The latter two changes are deemed to be of particular significance. Northern Ireland has been successful in terms of making structural institutional changes designed to accommodate and mediate difference. Key features of the 1998 Belfast Agreement include the power-sharing Northern Ireland Executive, cross-community voting and North–South bodies. Crucially however, the elite institutional creations have not led to broader change in terms of the structure of competition between communal blocs. The two communities in Northern Ireland continue to live apart. Relations have certainly softened, but mutual trust remains problematic. Fundamental disputes related to political aspirations remain intact and visions of a shared future do not exist, despite attempts to nurture them. Key features of society continue to be segregated, including the educational system, and legacy issues remain highly contentious. It was against this tenuous backdrop that Northern Ireland voters were asked to consider Britain's relationship with the EU, and ultimately the UK's constitutional future.

The build-up to the 2016 EU referendum in Northern Ireland

The 2016 EU referendum provided the second opportunity during the period of UK membership for citizens to pass judgement on the merits or otherwise of being part of the EU. A referendum in June 1975 – promised by the newly elected Labour Party Prime Minister Harold Wilson – put the question of continued UK membership of the then EEC to the British public. Northern Ireland's 52.1 per cent vote in favour of staying in the EU was a narrow victory for the Yes side, albeit one based on a low turnout of 48.2 per cent (see Bristow 1975). It also contrasted with the much higher turnout for the rest of the UK, which produced an emphatic 67.2 per cent Yes vote in favour of continued membership of the EEC. The SDLP and the Alliance Party of Northern Ireland (APNI) supported continued EEC membership, as did the Vanguard Unionists. In contrast, the DUP, most of the UUP, and Sinn Féin favoured a UK exit. The unionist position was informed by their opposition to any dilution of British sovereignty. For the DUP, religious objections to the Roman Catholic Church and its perceived links to the European project were a hallmark of the anti-EEC rhetoric of DUP leader, Rev Dr Ian Paisley (see Ganiel 2009: 578). John Hume, leader of the nationalist SDLP, was strongly supportive of the EEC. His suggestion that membership would challenge the logic for long-term partition of the island of Ireland unnerved unionists and arguably hardened their opposition. Sinn Féin opposed membership of the EEC too, and for similar reasons to their unionist counterparts. The party feared that membership of the Community would erode Irish sovereignty and challenge Irish culture and the Irish language. The republican position was also influenced by left-wing ideology, which viewed the EEC as a "rich man's club". The business community in Northern Ireland also largely supported the Yes campaign, as did a key Northern Ireland interest group, the Ulster Farmers' Union (UFU).

In 1975, the referendum followed seven votes in the previous two years in Northern Ireland. Voter weariness and fatigue was clearly a factor that impacted negatively on turnout. In addition, the Northern Ireland Troubles were at their most intense during the mid 1970s. The year 1975 was one of the deadliest years of the conflict, when violence claimed over 250 lives and tensions between the two communities were high. Against this backdrop, the EEC was an issue of secondary concern for many Northern Ireland voters. Moreover, the European focus of the referendum debate was unsuccessful in allowing the Northern Ireland political parties to free themselves from constitutional disputes and to overcome their domestic political differences (Greer 2016): "At the height of the Troubles, with the constitutional future of the North apparently up for grabs, many feared that European integration threatened both their preferred independent nation-states – a united Ireland or a maintained UK."

Almost 40 years later, the 2016 referendum revisited the same constitutional questions in Northern Ireland, which, although they had been relieved of some of their virulence by the peace process, nonetheless remained contested.

Clashing interests: The promise of a referendum and the Northern Ireland peace process

The decision by Conservative Party leader David Cameron to promise and then convene a referendum on UK membership of the EU exposes a fundamental clash between Conservative Party politics and the Northern Ireland peace process. What suited the political and electoral ambitions of the Tory Party, posed challenges for a precarious peace in Northern Ireland. The EU referendum exposed a troubling disconnect between the UK political centre and its most peripheral region, and it did so in a number of ways. The referendum question, the timing of the vote, the substance of the campaign and the atmosphere it created jarred with Northern Ireland's "negative peace".

First, the simplicity of the referendum question, which asked voters to choose between the UK leaving the EU or remaining in the EU, obscures the complexity and contentiousness of the constitutional issues such a question raises: "the 2016 in/out referendum meant asking UK voters to resolve a constitutional question of a complexity comparable only to 'the Irish Question', which convulsed British party politics in the nineteenth and early twentieth century" (Glencross 2016: 10). The EU referendum touched on profound political and constitutional questions in that it implicitly asked the electorate to make a judgement about the future of British sovereignty. This represented a complex and abstract challenge for voters. There has long been confusion around the precise meaning of national sovereignty in the UK, and in particular the internal (i.e. parliamentary sovereignty) and external (i.e. place and role within the international order) dimensions of the concept. Sovereignty also has an emotive and intangible nature, which is open to manipulation and exploitation. Gordon (2016: 333) notes: "the (attempted) reconciliation of national ideas of sovereignty with membership of the EU has been a source of enduring angst in parts of the UK's political establishment (and indeed, perhaps the referendum result suggests, in a substantial section of the electorate)".

Asking voters to consider the UK's sovereign future demands a campaign characterized by sophisticated analysis and debate. It should be accessible to voters, grounded in fact, free from rhetoric and honest about the multi-dimensional impact of a remain or leave decision. However, EU referendum campaigns rarely demonstrate such features or achieve such clarity. A glance at other member states' experience of referendums highlights that referendums on European integration are often highly unpredictable affairs.[2] Voters often employ "punishment strategies" and reject the positions taken by government, even when those positions are supported by most mainstream political parties, interest groups and experts (see Hobolt 2009, 2016). Education levels, attachment to nation, perceptions of people from other cultures, and socio-economic factors all impact on attitudes and emotions towards European integration. Reliance solely on a cost-benefit analysis, therefore, is not a sufficiently robust, comprehensive or impactful means to persuade voters to choose for or against EU membership. Such an approach overlooks some of the vital ways in which the vote has the potential to produce specific political and constitutional outcomes.

David Cameron may not have sufficiently appreciated the ways in which the notion, meaning and practice of national sovereignty could be hijacked and manipulated by those opposed to immigration, particularly in England. For other parts of the UK, the sovereignty issue had a different context. In Scotland, voters were sensitized to discussions around national sovereignty. The 2014 independence referendum had allowed Scottish voters to debate the meaning and implications of a (post-)sovereignty settlement for an independent Scotland. Both

---

2. There have been over 50 referendums on various aspects of European integration, including accession, treaty ratification and policy issues. Despite being among the more Europhile of EU member states, Irish voters have twice rejected EU treaty reforms in national referendums. In 2000 and again in 2008, the Irish electorate opposed first the Treaty of Nice and then the Treaty of Lisbon. Both decisions were later overturned when Irish voters voted for a second time on the back of legal and political guarantees and reassurances.

the Yes and No campaigns suggested that Scotland, in or out of the UK, would remain part of the EU. In Northern Ireland, the idea of national sovereignty has highly contested political connotations and is largely understood in terms of a choice between a United Kingdom and a united Ireland. The referendum placed discussion of the EU within that disputed space and opened up an arena where the contested "Irish question" could be revisited, rehashed and possibly revised (depending on the referendum outcome). The wider UK referendum campaign largely ignored the Irish dimension to the referendum. David Cameron's Chief Press Officer for Europe and Economic Affairs notes that Ireland was not afforded prominence in terms of campaign strategy (O'Toole 2017). Similarly, the Vote Leave campaign had little to say about Northern Ireland, other than to dismiss warnings about the border issue as "scaremongering".

For all these reasons, the content, subject and packaging of the referendum question was challenging for Northern Ireland, but so too was its timing. In calling the 2016 referendum, David Cameron appears to have given little, if any thought, to how the timing of such a referendum would play out in Northern Ireland. The "negative peace" there created a challenging backdrop against which to conduct a potentially polarizing debate on Brexit. A referendum campaign that involved discussion of emotive principles and constitutional choices, but in a context where communities did not fully trust each other, did not offer a constructive basis for mature dialogue. For Northern Ireland, the referendum campaign asked the two communities to confront issues that exposed deep-seated differences between them. The existence of a "negative peace" curtailed the region's ability to find a safe space where politicians and voters could prudently and dispassionately discuss issues that touched on sensitive constitutional questions for both nationalists and unionists.

The electoral prelude to the EU referendum: The 2016 Northern Ireland Assembly election

Seven weeks prior to the EU referendum, voters were again at the polls to vote in the Northern Ireland Assembly election. Elections in Northern Ireland have tended to be set-piece affairs. The key battle is often within the unionist and nationalist blocs, rather than between them. This is a feature of the distinctive dual ethnic party system that has shaped party politics in Northern Ireland since the 1980s (see Mitchell 1991, 1995, 1999). Ethnic parties tend only to seek electoral support from voters on "their side", that is nationalist political parties target nationalist (often Catholic) support while unionist political parties target unionist (often Protestant) voters. Within each communal bloc – nationalist and unionist – political rivalry between parties is often intense; the most vicious battles take place between parties that share the same political and constitutional aspirations. The key election talking points have traditionally concerned the means to achieve these aspirations. A particularly troublesome feature of the dual ethnic party system is that there are few incentives for moderate parties to reach across the communal divide for fear of being accused of "selling out". Additionally, in Northern Ireland politics, "middle-ground" parties that do not target one community over another have traditionally been unable to attract a credible cross-community vote. Collectively, the APNI, Green Party, the (now defunct) Northern Ireland Women's Coalition and the People Before Profit Alliance (PBPA) typically secure about 10 per cent of the popular vote. This type of party system can perpetuate the division of the communities by limiting the opportunities for parties to extend their appeal across the community divide. A concentration on constitutional issues also limits the space for (common) socio-economic policy challenges faced by both communities regardless of their political hue. Such debate tends to be side-lined. At election time, the dual ethnic party system is invariably about "getting the vote out", an approach that amounts to little more than an electoral contest that produces a "sectarian headcount" (see Mitchell 1999).

In the context of the evolving peace process, there were hopes that strong communal identities would dissipate and that the toxicity of the dual ethnic party system would diminish. Twenty years later communalism continues but there are signs that the dual ethnic party system is being challenged. The more extreme elements within each communal bloc – namely the DUP and Sinn Féin – have moderated their positions and some progress has resulted (McGlynn *et al.* 2014: 276): "whilst ethnic outbidding exerts a strong pull over parties and their electoral strategies, attempts to explore more expansive visions of political and national identity within Northern Ireland have been more evident in recent years".

There has also been some small increase in voters opting to identify as Northern Irish (rather than British or Irish), and in addition, recent election campaigns have seen greater discussion of economic and social issues as well as political and constitutional questions. In a sign of progress, the 2016 election campaign included some discussion of social issues. The election, however, also demonstrated the resilience of the dual ethnic party system, although the salience of the ethno-national divide did appear to be less apparent in 2016 than in previous elections. The 2016 Assembly election campaign also coincided with the run-up to the 2016 EU referendum and offered a space for discussion of the looming EU constitutional question. However, despite the imminent (and important) vote, "the subject failed to garner much attention from the local parties until after the Assembly campaign" (Matthews & Pow 2017: 317).

The election results were unsurprising. On a relatively low turnout of 54.2 per cent, individual parties' share of the vote remained pretty stable. The DUP had a good election. The party held on to its 38 seats to emerge again as the largest party in Northern Ireland. Their main competitor, Sinn Féin, was down one seat to 28 and sustained a drop in its vote share. This was the first time that Sinn Féin had not increased its vote share and for some commentators, was interpreted as a sign of electoral stagnation. The smaller unionist party, the UUP, did not sustain losses but nor did it make any of the gains predicted during the campaign. It was a disappointing election for the nationalist SDLP, which shed two seats. The middle-ground parties achieved some success. The APNI held onto its eight seats, while the Green Party doubled its seat share to two, and for the first time, the PBPA[3] entered the Assembly with two seats. Although UKIP did contest the Northern Ireland Assembly election, the sitting UKIP MLA chose not to contest his seat. The party won 1.5 per cent of the vote (double their vote share in 2011), but their presence in the Assembly was eliminated. The UK Conservative Party also fielded candidates but won just 0.4 per cent of the vote. The British Labour Party does not contest elections in Northern Ireland.

The electoral make-up of the 2016 Assembly was not emphatically different from its previous iteration (see Table 2.2), although in relative terms, there were small gains for the middle ground.

---

3. The PBPA is a small, left-wing, Eurosceptic party that is active in both Northern Ireland and the Republic of Ireland. Created in 2005, the party favours a 32-county socialist Republic, but its primary emphasis is on the pursuit of its socialist agenda.

Table 2.2 Northern Ireland Assembly election results 2016

Party	Seats	Vote share	Remain/Leave
DUP	38	29.2%	Leave
Sinn Féin	28 (-1)	24.0%	Remain
UUP	16	12.6%	Remain
SDLP	12 (-2)	12.0%	Remain
APNI	8	7.0%	Remain
Green Party	2 (+1)	2.7%	Remain
PBPA	2 (+2)	2.0%	Leave
TUV	1	3.4%	Leave
Independents	1	3.3%	Remain

During the Northern Ireland Assembly election campaign, discussion of the EU referendum was minimal. However, the position of all of the parties on the referendum question was known (see Table 2.2). Three parties – accounting for 41 seats or 28 per cent of Assembly representation – advocated a Leave position. The DUP and TUV, both unionist Eurosceptic parties on the right of the political spectrum, and the small, socialist and Eurosceptic PBPA, were strongly in favour of Leave. The parties advocating for Remain were drawn from a variety of political backgrounds, including unionist, nationalist and middle-ground, and espoused a number of different political outlooks, including social democracy, green, centre-right and centre-left.

The Assembly election provided an indicator of how the Brexit referendum might unfold in Northern Ireland. A strong Remain vote appeared likely. This was largely reinforced by a series of opinion polls from August 2015 that consistently demonstrated majority support for Remain in Northern Ireland (see Table 2.3). Interestingly, the final two polls before the referendum date suggested that as the vote drew nearer, support for Remain was wavering and support for Leave increasing.[4]

The Assembly election result and opinion polling suggested a reasonably static level of support for Remain in the weeks and months

---

4. The timing of these two polls is important. The fieldwork was conducted in June 2016 during the late stages of the referendum campaign when the debate on Brexit was at its height.

Table 2.3 Selection of EU referendum opinion polls for Northern Ireland 2015–16*

Poll	Remain	Leave	Undecided/ Not voting
Lucidtalk Northern Ireland Opinion Panel Polling, June 2016	52%	38%	10%
Millward Brown Ulster Poll, 15 June 2016	48%	32%	20%
Lucidtalk Northern Ireland Opinion Panel Polling, May 2016	54%	35%	11%
Millward Brown Ulster Poll, 19 May 2016	55%	23%	22%
Lucidtalk Northern Ireland Opinion Panel Polling, April 2016	54%	34%	12%
Danske Bank Poll, March 2016	56%	18%	26%
Lucidtalk Northern Ireland Opinion Panel Polling, March 2016	60%	33%	7%
Belfast Telegraph BIG100 Online Poll, 22 February 2016	55%	29%	15%
Belfast Telegraph BIG60 Online Poll, 6 November 2015	56%	28%	18%
Behaviour and Attitudes (RTÉ and BBC Northern Ireland), 16 October 2015	55%	13%	32%
Danske Bank Poll, 5 August 2015	58%	16%	26%

* Due to rounding, not all results will total 100%.

prior to the referendum. Just one of the polls (Millward Brown Ulster Poll, June 2016) identified less than 50 per cent support for Remain. The average of the poll findings over the period August 2015 to June 2016 is 54.8 per cent, which is 1 per cent less than the actual referendum result. The key difference between the polling figures and the actual result is the increase in support for a UK exit from the EU. It appears that those who were undecided largely opted to vote Leave on 23 June 2016. An examination of the discourse and dynamics that animated the EU referendum campaign in Northern Ireland reveals what forces were present, how they influenced the outcome and the extent to which they politicized the Brexit issue and polarized voters.

The EU referendum campaign in Northern Ireland

Voter attitudes towards the EU are aided and shaped by a series of factors. Hooghe and Marks (2005) note three primary ways in which public attitudes towards Europe are formed. Voters are influenced by their evaluation of the economic consequences of the EU for individuals and for one's state, and by their view on the impact of the EU on communal identities. In addition, voters take note of cues from political parties, from political leaders and from their own ideological predispositions. According to Clarke *et al.* (2017: 446): "Research on how cues affect public attitudes towards the EU emphasizes the roles of political parties and party leaders." In Northern Ireland, political parties' attitudes towards the EU have tended to follow predictable communal lines.

Predictable positions: Northern Ireland's political parties and the EU referendum

Nationalists in Northern Ireland have traditionally been more supportive of the European integration project than unionists. The most Europhile of political parties is the nationalist SDLP. The party's support for the EU can be traced to the foundations of the SDLP in the early 1970s. One of its earliest policy documents references the then EEC as a model for political reconciliation. From the SDLP perspective however, political reconciliation in Northern Ireland was understood as a journey towards a united Ireland with the EU providing an important context within which to achieve Irish unity (McLoughlin 2009: 605): "In articulating a peaceful, gradualist approach to Irish reunification, the party frequently cited postwar Europe as an example of how former antagonists could overcome their differences through a process of cooperation in areas of common social and economic interest."

Unionists have been cynical about the SDLP position on the EU. The UUP, for example, was completely opposed to any attempts by the SDLP to link the resolution of the Northern Ireland conflict with the EU. Murphy (2009: 593) notes: "talk of such a possibility tended to further harden UUP attitudes to Europe". It also served to reinforce the EU divide between unionism and nationalism.

In 2016, the SDLP was a strong and early advocate of the Remain position. The party viewed Brexit as being disastrous for Northern Ireland political, economic and social interests (McCann & Hainsworth 2017: 329). The SDLP was vociferous and vocal in calling for the UK to stay in the EU. Their campaign position was clear and unequivocal.

Not all Irish nationalists, however, were comfortable with membership of the EU. Sinn Féin has traditionally been much more critical of the EU than the SDLP. In the years both before and after UK and Irish accession to the EU, the party was hostile towards the European integration project and completely opposed to EU membership for Ireland. Sinn Féin saw EU membership as an economic disaster and an imperialist threat for the whole island of Ireland (Maillot 2009: 560). The party's hostility towards the EU began to moderate, particularly from the 1990s. The Sinn Féin European message became more sophisticated as the party identified a critical approach to the EU that was less inimical to the EU than the Eurosceptic positions being espoused by its unionist rivals. Sinn Féin's critical engagement with EU issues became apparent during the Treaty of Nice, Treaty of Lisbon and Fiscal Treaty referendum campaigns in the Republic of Ireland. On all three occasions, the party campaigned for a No vote. This opposition to EU treaty reform "gave the party the opportunity to brand itself as a strong defender of neutrality, sovereignty and left-wing ideals" (Maillot 2009: 567). The fact that Sinn Féin was one of few critical voices in calling for a No vote gave the party an important platform, one that allowed it to develop a profile that offered voters a radical but credible alternative. The party's opposition to the EU, however, is not outright and this was apparent from late 2015 when a party strategy paper on Europe committed Sinn Féin to oppose a UK exit from the EU (McCann & Hainsworth 2017: 328). The party was opposed to Brexit for the negative impact it would have on all-Ireland affairs, on the Belfast Agreement and on access to EU funding. This clear messaging formed the unambiguous core of the Sinn Féin position on Brexit.

Unionists in Northern Ireland have generally been less enthusiastic about the EU and the European integration process. The DUP has consistently adopted a Eurosceptic position. Originally this position was heavily grounded in extreme religious objections to the purpose of European integration. Former DUP leader, Rev Dr Ian Paisley, was ardently opposed to the Roman Catholic ethos of the EU. The party also objected to the manner in which EU membership implied a dilution of British national sovereignty. Such concerns "touch on issues of British identity which are, of course, vital to unionist opinion" (Ganiel 2009: 581). The party was also stridently opposed to the EU's single currency, the euro. This hardcore opposition to the EU, however, has not prevented the DUP from engaging with EU issues and EU institutions (most notably the EP). The party has returned a DUP representative to the EP in every European election since 1979.[5] The DUP has welcomed the funding available to Northern Ireland from the EU and has supported Northern Ireland agricultural interests in Brussels. The DUP's decision to support the Leave position in 2016 was unsurprising when considered in the context of the party's longstanding opposition to the EU. However, it was nevertheless a curious positon to adopt given the negative impact Brexit was predicted to have on Northern Ireland generally, and specifically on the farming community, a large DUP constituency. An overall UK-wide Leave vote was also viewed as a development that could reinforce calls for a second Scottish independence referendum and so potentially destabilize the political unity of the UK. This would be a worrying prospect for a party strongly wedded to the unionist ideal. There was some acknowledgment by DUP party leader, Arlene Foster, that party supporters may have reservations about Brexit (DUP 2016a): "we will on balance recommend a vote to leave the EU. Importantly however, the decision on whether the United Kingdom should remain in or leave the EU is fundamentally not one for parties but for every individual voter across the nation to determine".

This ambiguous messaging is problematic. The DUP position left some room for party members and voters to opt for Remain. A lack of clarity from the party leader played out in terms of two contrasting approaches to campaigning. Two key DUP figures, Sammy Wilson and Ian Paisley Jnr, were very visible and audible during the campaign. Wilson shared a stage in Belfast in March 2016 with leading UK Brexiteers including UKIP leader Nigel Farage and Labour Party MP Kate Hoey. Other DUP party members were less engaged and more

---

5. DUP candidate, Jim Allister, won an EP seat in 2004, but he left the party during the parliamentary term. He subsequently formed the Traditional Unionist Voice (TUV) party and lost his seat to the DUP in 2009.

muted in their approach to campaigning. Mixed messaging from the party leadership may go some way to explaining why the number of undecideds remained consistently high in Northern Ireland opinion polls. In the absence of clear and unambiguous cues from their political leaders, DUP voters may have struggled to settle on a Remain/Leave position. The very small TUV party was vehemently opposed to the EU and, like the DUP, it too supported the UK leaving the EU.

Unlike the DUP and TUV, the UUP opted to support the Remain position. The UUP's relationship with the EU has been less hostile than the DUP's. However, during the early years of UK and Irish membership of the EU, the party was opposed to the EU. This hostility was "grounded in a fear of the erosion of the sovereignty of the Westminster parliament and a belief that any form of internationalization will aid nationalists in Northern Ireland" (Murphy 2009: 593). The UUP's opposition to the EU has, however, moderated over time. The party's long-time MEP, Jim Nicholson,[6] has consistently labelled himself a "Euro-realist". This relates to a vision of the EU that "focuses on common sense regulation rather than red tape, promotes business rather than bureaucracy, and reduces expenditure rather than spending to excess – a reformed EU that works in your best interests" (UUP 2014: 4). The UUP was the last of the Northern Ireland parties to declare its position on the EU referendum. It did so in March 2016 (UUP 2016a):

> The Ulster Unionist Party believes that on balance Northern Ireland is better remaining in the European Union, with the UK Government pressing for further reform and a return to the founding principle of free trade, not greater political union. The party respects that individual members may vote for withdrawal on the 23rd of June.

Like the DUP, however, the UUP was ambiguous in its messaging. The party advocated a Remain position, but accepted that individual members may vote Leave. Current and former UUP members expressed

---

6. Jim Nicholson has been a UUP MEP since 1989. He sits with the European Conservatives and Reformists Group in the European Parliament. Fellow MEPs in this political grouping include British Conservative Party members.

differing opinions on the referendum vote and there were reservations about the party's approach. The party leadership was openly challenged by senior party veterans, including former UUP leader Lord David Trimble and former party grandees Lord Kilclooney and Lord Maginnis. In an open letter to *The News Letter* (17 June 2016), they wrote: "We write to appeal to all Ulster Unionists to vote to leave the European Union on 23 June … A vote to leave on 23 June is a vote for confidence in the United Kingdom". The letter expresses concern at the direction of the European integration process and calls for the restoration of British sovereignty. The signatories reject the "dishonest scaremongering" that a vote to leave would jeopardize the Northern Ireland peace process and they express faith in the robustness of the institutions and structures created by the Belfast Agreement. Current UUP members were also hesitant about voting Remain. Ex-party leader and then MP, Tom Elliott, openly admitted that he was unsure about how to cast his vote. These positions contrast with the party leader's strong support for the UK to stay in the EU. In his evidence to the House of Commons Northern Ireland Affairs Committee inquiry into the EU referendum in Northern Ireland, then UUP leader, Mike Nesbitt, queried the impact of Brexit on the loss of EU economic support for farmers, the community and voluntary sectors, industry and education (Evidence Session, 7 March 2016). He expressed concerns about the impact on the border between Northern Ireland and the Republic of Ireland, and the existential threat that a UK exit from the EU might pose. Overall, UUP supporters were subjected to contrasting and contradictory perspectives and analyses from senior party figures. The lack of party unity on the EU referendum question further complicated an already complex debate.

Mobilizing parties and motivating voters: Differing Unionist and Nationalist approaches

Recent research suggests that cues alone are not enough in terms of motivating voters. In a study of how cueing effects depend on both the strength of party identification and the degree of exposure to campaign material, Azrout and de Vreese (2017: 12) find: "if parties wish to persuade their constituencies, they really need to put in the effort to reach them". This underlines the importance of political parties engaging robustly with election and referendum campaigns. Where engagement is limited and messaging ambiguous, voters may be less motivated to vote and less inclined to know how best to vote to protect their interests.

The EU referendum in Northern Ireland provoked different reactions from the unionist and nationalist blocs. Nationalism, as represented by Sinn Féin and the SDLP, strongly and confidently supported Remain. The nationalist political community was largely united in its opposition to the UK leaving the EU.[7] The broad basis for that opposition – the perceived negative economic and political impact of Brexit on Northern Ireland and on all-island relations – was shared by both political parties. The parties' position on the referendum question was rationalized in the context of their position on the Irish constitutional question, and particularly the store they placed in protecting North–South relations on the island of Ireland. Being able to clearly connect EU and national preferences lent strength, depth and persuasiveness to the nationalist preference for Remain. Nationalism articulated and delivered a clear message to their voting base, which the vast majority of their supporters heeded. In contrast, unionism, as represented by the UUP, DUP and TUV, was much more polarized on the question of continued UK membership of the EU. The TUV was manifestly and unapologetically in favour of Brexit. Officially, the DUP supported Leave although the extent to which this position was actively promoted by party members varied. The UUP's official position was to recommend support for Remain, but the party was clearly split on the issue. The different unionist interpretations of the impact of Brexit on the UK and on Northern Ireland presented voters with a confusing choice. The inconsistency in the messaging meant that the question of how best to use the referendum to protect the broader unionist preference (for the maintenance of the constitutional link between Northern Ireland and Britain) was highly unclear to voters. Unionists might have looked to the British government and the Conservative Party for cues, but here too division was evident. The position adopted by the then

---

7. An exception to this was the small Republican dissident group, Éirígí (Gaelic for "rising"), which is supported by disaffected Sinn Féin members who disagreed with the party's move towards a compromise with unionism during the 1990s. The party's strong opposition to the EU motivated support for Brexit.

Secretary of State for Northern Ireland muddied the referendum waters even further.

Contradictory messages: The Conservative Party and the EU referendum in Northern Ireland

Conservative Party MP and Secretary of State for Northern Ireland, Theresa Villiers, was one of four full members of the British cabinet who chose to reject the party line and to campaign in favour of Brexit.[8] This put her at odds not just with her own prime minister, but also with most political parties in Northern Ireland, and with the Irish government, which was urging a Remain vote. The secretary of state's decision to support Leave was motivated by the negative impact of the EU on British national sovereignty. As a former MEP, Theresa Villiers regards the EU as "unreformable" and she views membership of the EU as incompatible with the UK's best interests (Villiers 2016a). Throughout the campaign, the secretary of state denied that Brexit would require the imposition of a hard border between Northern Ireland and the Republic of Ireland and claimed that the border would continue to be free-flowing. She also rejected the idea that Brexit might have the potential to destabilize the Northern Ireland peace process. She accused those with such views as engaging in unnecessary and irresponsible scare-mongering. Villiers also asserted that the end of UK contributions to the EU budget would allow for current EU funding to Northern Ireland, including agricultural support, to continue but to come directly from the British Exchequer (see Villiers 2016b).

The secretary of state's decision to support the Leave campaign signalled a subtle shift in the established British–Irish bilateral approach to Northern Ireland affairs. This approach has been carefully cultivated since the 1990s and has played an important role in facilitating the peace process. During that decade, British–Irish relations *vis-à-vis* Northern Ireland developed to the point where traditional policy positions evolved and allowed for bilateral consensus on resolving the conflict to emerge (see Tannam 2011). This type of cooperation was instrumental in paving the way for agreement on the 1998 Belfast Agreement

---

8. Her predecessor, Owen Patterson, also supported the Leave vote.

and on subsequent agreements including the St Andrew's Agreement (2006), the Hillsborough Agreement (2010) and the Stormont House Agreement (2014).[9] The continuation of close and constructive relations between the two governments since 1998 has been a fundamentally important component in sustaining the peace process. During difficult and challenging periods, the two governments have been able to present a united front in their dealings with the Northern Ireland political parties. The British–Irish axis increasingly presented shared preferences as to possible solutions in dealing with crises. The strength of this approach often proved decisive in forcing the parties to seek and achieve political accommodation.

Theresa Villiers's decision to vote and campaign for Brexit meant that the British government was divided on a key Northern Ireland issue with potentially harmful economic, political and constitutional implications. The lack of unity between the Irish government and the British government's representative in Northern Ireland was one of the first times in many years that bi-national consensus on a key Northern Ireland issue had not prevailed. The consequences of such a development should not be underestimated. It meant that Northern Ireland's British government representative shared the same position as hard-line unionist parties, the DUP and TUV. The Irish government was supportive of the position adopted by nationalism, but that position also represented the official views of the UUP and middle-ground parties such as the APNI. Irish support for Remain also aligned with the UK prime minister's preference. The absence of a strong accord between the British and Irish governments on a highly sensitive constitutional question disturbed an established consensus-based modus operandi for British–Irish relations when dealing with sensitive Northern Ireland issues. This created some tensions between the two administrations. The Irish government's singular focus on pushing for a Remain vote meant an inevitable clash with the Northern Ireland Secretary of State. There were a number of incidences during the referendum campaign when she and the then Irish Minister for Foreign Affairs and Trade,

---

9. These agreements dealt with issues that had not been fully resolved by the Belfast Agreement. They included the devolution of justice and policing powers, and a range of other political, social and economic issues.

Charlie Flanagan, contradicted each other, particularly in relation to their differing views about the status of the border in the event of Brexit. British–Irish unity on how best to protect Northern Ireland's future was weakened by this breakdown in consensus and cooperation.

Theresa Villiers was not the only British Conservative Party figure to be out of step with the prime minister's position. Party maverick and the then Mayor of London, Boris Johnson, also visited Northern Ireland in early 2016 and echoed Villiers's comments that border arrangements between Northern Ireland and the Republic of Ireland would not change following a UK withdrawal from the EU (BBC News, 29 February 2016). His views reflected those of UKIP leader, Nigel Farage, who was a regular visitor to Northern Ireland during the referendum campaign. Prime Minister David Cameron also spent time in Northern Ireland during the referendum campaign. During those visits, he disagreed with the analysis of his secretary of state in relation to the impact of Brexit on the border and on agriculture in Northern Ireland. At the most senior UK government level, the interpretation of what a vote to Leave would mean was unclear. There was even less clarity apparent at the level of the devolved Northern Ireland institutions.

Leadership lacking: The Northern Ireland Executive and the EU referendum

The varied positions adopted by the different political parties in Northern Ireland meant that it was impossible for the Executive to produce an agreed position on the EU referendum question. The multi-party make-up of the power-sharing Executive comprised representatives from the APNI, DUP, SDLP, Sinn Féin and the UUP. Given that parties supported both the Remain and Leave campaigns, it was always unlikely that the Executive would reach any sort of agreement as to how to position Northern Ireland on Brexit. This contrasted with the approach of the SNP-led Scottish government, which supported Remain, and the Welsh Labour Party minority government, which also supported Remain. In both cases, each government was campaigning for the UK to stay in the EU and depicting this option as being in the best interests of the regions. No such cues were available in Northern Ireland. The Executive offered no analysis of the implications of Brexit for Northern Ireland. It is possible (even likely) that the Northern

Ireland Executive did not discuss the EU referendum at all in the lead up to the vote. Although the Executive does not routinely publish the minutes of its meetings, senior civil servants in Northern Ireland suggest that there was no discussion of Brexit around the Executive table. To do so risked opening up divisions and politicians of all hues were loath to this possibility. Publications produced by the Northern Ireland Executive during this period are also weak in their consideration of the referendum issue. A key government document, the Northern Ireland Programme for Government was not fully finalized before the suspension of the Northern Ireland devolved institutions in early 2017. The *Draft Programme for Government Framework 2016–2021* (published 26 May 2016), however, did not reference the referendum or include any contingency about how Northern Ireland might deal with a Leave vote. In fact, the document appears to have been blind to the possibility of Brexit as it includes reference to EU funding, EU legislation and the European Commission's Trans-European Transport Network for Northern Ireland. During a Northern Ireland Assembly debate on the Programme for Government, the late Deputy First Minister Martin McGuinness noted: "The way that I look at it is that the referendum will be over on 23 June and that we will deal with the aftermath of that when it comes" (Official Report, 9 March 2016). A similar perspective was evident from the DUP. In response to a question concerning the future of EU Peace funding in the event of Brexit, DUP Minister for Finance and Personnel, Mervyn Storey, responded (Official Report, 8 March 2016):

> Now that we have the call open for the new [EU] Peace funding … I want to see organisations right across [Northern Ireland] making applications that can stand scrutiny and pass the test so that we can build upon the good successful projects, and … maximize the money that has come, albeit that we might like to have more money in the future. That is a debate, I believe, for when we know the outcome of the referendum.

This political disinclination to talk about the EU referendum is all the more surprising given that the Northern Ireland Executive's *International Relations Strategy* (2014) notes: "The Executive has a special and important relationship with the European Union particularly for economic and social programmes" (Paragraph 5.1). The glaring absence of any mention of the referendum in the draft Programme for Government coupled with political hesitation in terms of discussing the referendum hints at how reluctant the Northern Ireland Executive was to engage with the Brexit question in the weeks and months before the vote.

Limited engagement: The Northern Ireland Assembly and the EU referendum

The Northern Ireland Assembly was an alternative site for considering the referendum question, and there was some attempt by Assembly committees to discuss the potential impact of Brexit on Northern Ireland. In 2015, the Enterprise, Trade and Investment Committee commissioned a study examining the consequences of Brexit for the Northern Ireland economy (see Budd 2015). It stands as one of the only detailed analyses of how Brexit might affect Northern Ireland's economic future (this is discussed in greater detail in Chapter 3).[10] Similar to the Executive however, Assembly committees were generally reluctant to discuss the EU referendum for fear of opening up uncomfortable political and constitutional conversations. The Committee of the Executive Office, for example, has responsibility for overseeing and scrutinizing the work of the Executive Office, but the committee did not engage to any extensive degree with the referendum issue. Of course, there was little for the committee to scrutinize given the absence of a Northern Ireland Executive position on the referendum. This lack of engagement with the EU referendum extended to other committees. No Northern Ireland Assembly committee inquiry was conducted into the possible implications of a Leave vote for Northern Ireland. Sources suggest that there was a discernible reluctance among MLAs to examine impact and evidence, because even practical discussions had the potential to polarize parties and to lead to deep political tensions. The DUP, in particular, was opposed to Assembly inquiries, although the UUP was generally more pragmatic about seeking evidence.

---

10. In 2016, the Assembly's Research and Information Service also published a research paper *The EU Referendum and Potential Implications for Northern Ireland*, which focused largely on trade and investment.

In terms of Assembly questions, there were only 19 questions asked during the 2015/2016 Assembly session that referenced the referendum or Brexit. Most questions were posed by SDLP and Sinn Féin MLAs, with just one question each asked by APNI MLA Trevor Lunn and TUV leader Jim Allister.[11] The bulk of the questions queried the date of the referendum so close to the Assembly elections (taking place in May 2016) and asked about what preparations the Northern Ireland Executive was making in the event of a UK vote to leave the EU. The responses from ministers suggested that there was little in the way of contingency planning taking place across government departments.

The limited attention to the EU referendum by the Northern Ireland Assembly is in rather striking contrast to the efforts of other parliamentary institutions that dedicated considerably more energy to examinations of the potential consequences of Brexit for Northern Ireland. The House of Commons Northern Ireland Affairs Committee[12] conducted a wide-ranging inquiry into the issues affecting Northern Ireland in respect of the EU referendum. The terms of reference for the inquiry outlined that the aim was "to inform and encourage public debate in Northern Ireland ahead of the referendum". The committee's report, *Northern Ireland and the EU Referendum*, was published approximately one month before the vote and focused mainly on issues of trade, the border, EU funding and agriculture.

The Irish parliament (Houses of the Oireachtas) was similarly active in engaging with the referendum issue. In 2015, the Joint Committee on European Union Affairs produced a report, *UK/EU Future Relationship: Implications for Ireland*. The committee undertook to examine the issue because members considered: "the status of the UK's membership with the EU, and any change in that status, to be of such importance to Ireland, that it was incumbent on the Committee to examine this issue and report on our findings, from an Irish perspective" (Joint Committee on European Union Affairs 2015: 4). The report included a section

---

11. There was more than a five-fold increase in the number of Brexit-related questions put to ministers after the referendum vote.
12. The Northern Ireland Affairs Committee has 13 members, five of whom were Northern Ireland MPs in 2016 – two DUP, one SDLP, one UUP and one Independent. Sinn Féin has an abstentionist policy in relation to Westminster and Sinn Féin MPs do not take their seats in the House of Commons. However, party members did give oral evidence to the committee's inquiry.

dedicated to Northern Ireland and the potential negative impact of a UK vote to exit the EU on North–South relations, on cross-border institutions and on the border.

Civil society restraint: Cautious engagement with the EU referendum in Northern Ireland

In the absence of strong political input from within Northern Ireland, there was a space and opportunity for civil society to contribute to the referendum discussion. The main Northern Ireland social partners produced some guidance for their members (see Table 2.4). Trade unions and community and voluntary organizations in Northern Ireland were more likely to urge their members to support the Remain campaign. The Northern Ireland Public Services Association was highly unusual in advocating for Leave. Most civil society groups opted either to support

Table 2.4 Northern Ireland social partners and the EU referendum

Organization	Category	Referendum position
CBI Northern Ireland	Employer organization	Remain
Federation of Small Businesses (Northern Ireland)	Business organization	Neutral
Institute of Directors	Business organization	Neutral
Irish Congress of Trade Unions	Trade union	Remain
Manufacturing Northern Ireland	Business organization	Remain
Northern Ireland Chamber of Commerce and Industry	Business organization	Neutral
Northern Ireland Council for Voluntary Action (NICVA)	Voluntary and community sector	Remain
Northern Ireland Food and Drink Association	Business organization	Remain
Northern Ireland Independent Retail Trade Association	Business organization	Remain
Northern Ireland Public Service Association	Trade union	Leave
Trades Union Congress (TUC)	Trade union	Remain
Ulster Farmers' Union (UFU)	Farming organization	Neutral

Remain or to be neutral on the issue. The leading employer organization in Northern Ireland, the Confederation of British Industry (CBI), was supportive of the Remain position. Other business organizations, however, were more reticent in terms of seeking to influence voters, and some of them opted to be neutral on the referendum question. For those involved in the business sector, the messaging from their representative organizations was mixed.

Northern Ireland's largest farming organization, the UFU, also decided not to provide guidance to its members about how to vote. The union did facilitate discussion of the referendum, but UFU messaging was ambiguous. The organization's president, Barclay Bell, explained the reason for not pushing for either Remain or Leave (UFU 2016):

> As a Union we are not advising our members how to vote. We have said that in the absence of no compelling reason to leave, we see remaining as the safer option – but from the outset we have said our 12,000 plus members and their families will make up their own minds how to vote. This debate is wider than agriculture and it is our aim to create an opportunity for people to have their questions answered, before they finally cast their vote in what will almost certainly be a once in a generation referendum opportunity.

It is clear that there is a wide range of opinion among the 12,000 members of the UFU. In a telling contribution to the Northern Ireland Affairs Committee inquiry into Northern Ireland and the EU referendum (16 March 2016), the then president of the UFU noted:

> We see divides within sectors of our industry. We see splits within families within our membership. We have husbands and wives who are completely opposed on this. Again, the discussion in many households is about their head and their heart, because in their head the individuals think, "Look, we need market access. We need security. We need the surety of being members of this trade organisation," and their heart says, "We do not want to lose our UK identity. We do not want to lose autonomy." That is the dilemma. That is the discussion … we can see a difference of opinion.

This neatly captures the difficulty faced by a number of organizations in Northern Ireland during the EU referendum campaign. Fears of offending and alienating sections of their membership prevented them from articulating a definite position, and from rigorously promoting that position among their membership and more broadly. Being too strident in relation to the referendum question risked stoking political and communal tensions at the sectoral level. The economic impact of a possible Brexit could not be isolated from the political sensitivities felt by members on the referendum question. This appears to have been very much the case for Northern Ireland's farming sector.[13] The importance of the Common Agricultural Policy (CAP), the single farm payment and access to markets was not compelling enough a reason for many Northern Ireland farmers to vote Remain. Other concerns around sovereignty, "taking back control", EU regulation and the cost of membership were also important in influencing how farmers voted (see Kelly 2016). UFU membership is predominantly drawn from the "larger, productivist-oriented farms in the east [of Northern Ireland]" (Keating *et al.* 2009: 11). These holdings are typically associated with farmers from a Protestant background, many of whom vote DUP and UUP. For the UFU to articulate a policy position at odds with their membership's historic support for unionism was simply not possible or desirable.

The official Leave and Remain campaign groups were active in Northern Ireland. The Britain Stronger in Europe and Vote Leave organizations established branches in Northern Ireland and engaged in referendum discourse. The Vote Leave organization was closely associated with the DUP (see McCann & Hainsworth 2017: 333). EU Debate NI launched in late 2015 and adopted a neutral positon on the referendum question. The initiative was led by the Centre for Democracy and Peace Building (CDPB) and it endeavoured to provide a space for discussion of key referendum themes. EU Debate NI hosted a series of events and produced a briefing paper *To Remain or Leave? Northern Ireland and the EU Referendum*, which highlights some of the EU referendum issues that Northern Ireland voters were urged to consider in deciding how to vote. The media plays an important role

---

13. A straw poll of Northern Ireland farmers at a UFU EU referendum debate on 7 June 2016 opted to support Leave.

during any election or referendum campaign. Northern Ireland has its own local press, radio and television outlets, but there is strong penetration by the British press and media. British press and media coverage of the EU referendum tended to lean towards the pro-Leave position (see Curtice 2017). Unlike their British counterparts, the three main local daily newspapers in Northern Ireland did not take a position on the referendum. Anecdotally however, the nationalist *Irish News* was more critical of the Leave arguments.

Modest manoeuvring: EU referendum issues and dynamics in Northern Ireland

The EU referendum campaign in Northern Ireland was less dynamic and more muted than in other parts of the UK: "the debate in Northern Ireland has lacked the intensity that party politics in Westminster has given it" (House of Commons Northern Ireland Affairs Committee 2016: 3; see also Murphy 2016a and 2016b). This can be partly explained by the fact that the referendum campaign in Northern Ireland was considerably less hostile than it was in England. A functional and transactional relationship with the EU had for many years been the hallmark of Northern Ireland–EU relations. The depth and intensity of Euroscepticism is markedly less in Northern Ireland. Although the DUP has a Eurosceptic character, it is of the softer variety. This position has not prevented the party from engaging (sometimes enthusiastically) with EU policies and funding opportunities, and moreover, DUP opposition to the EU has not typically been framed around calls for the UK to leave the EU. A hard Eurosceptic voice has not traditionally been a feature of EU discourse in Northern Ireland – given their size, the anti-EU PBPA and TUV have limited political purchase in Northern Ireland, and nor are they a united Eurosceptic force. The two parties occupy opposite ends of the political spectrum and have contrasting positions on the constitutional question. UKIP was also a marginal voice during the referendum campaign in that the party does not have a strong political or electoral base in Northern Ireland. Similarly, the Conservative Party in Northern Ireland was a small player in the debate. As a consequence, the types of Eurosceptic issues that animated the wider UK referendum discussion, including immigration and British sovereignty, had limited traction in Northern Ireland.

The EU referendum campaign in Northern Ireland focused predominantly on the implications of Brexit for the border between Northern Ireland and the Republic of Ireland, free movement of people and trade and the impact of a UK exit on the fragile peace process. The question of EU funding, particularly future access to structural funds, the Peace Programme and the CAP, also featured in campaign debates. The issue of immigration – which so animated the campaign across England – was not a key talking point in Northern Ireland. For the most part, Remain supporters in Northern Ireland emphasized the detrimental effects of Leave on key economic sectors and they also expressed concerns about the impact of a possible Brexit on the peace process. In contrast, Leave campaigners disputed these dire economic warnings and did not link a UK exit from the EU with having any negative impact on North–South relations. Overall, the referendum campaign in Northern Ireland cast the debate around a straightforward cost-benefit analysis. Sinn Féin's Martin McGuinness did call on the British government to commit to holding a referendum on a united Ireland in the event of a UK vote to leave the EU (*Irish Times*, 11 March 2016), but overall, there were few attempts to delve into discussions about the repercussions of a Leave vote for the UK and Northern Ireland's future.

The constitutional issue that so divides unionist and nationalist communities in Northern Ireland was not substantially addressed by either Leavers or Remainers in the context of the UK's future within or without the EU. There was little appetite for talking about how an overall UK vote for Leave might challenge or alter the constitutional status quo in Northern Ireland. The delicate political balance in Northern Ireland was not sufficiently robust to countenance philosophical and constitutional examinations of the deeper meaning of EU membership for the UK and Ireland, and how this might connect with Northern Ireland's constitutional future. Such a discussion risked confronting unionists, and the DUP in particular, with challenging questions about how to accommodate Northern Ireland's best interests in the event of a Leave vote that precipitated the break-up of the UK.

For the most part, the referendum debate was largely divorced from traditional constitutional battles, and this made for a more muted and less hostile campaign. It meant that controversial and sensitive dimensions of the referendum discussion were circumvented, and a sharp confrontation between unionism and nationalism was avoided. This was possible because the Northern Ireland campaign did not *directly* confront difficult issues around British sovereignty, identity and the UK's constitutional future that were being aired elsewhere. Nevertheless, the reluctance of the Northern Ireland Executive and Assembly to consider the implications of a Leave vote and the broader shying away from sensitive political and constitutional themes, did not mean that tensions were avoided. The very fact that political parties were unwilling and unable to discuss such issues is testament to how challenging they remain for the two communities. This tainted political debate and undermined the extent to which mature political discussion and engagement was possible. Requiring Northern Ireland political parties and leaders to deal with highly complex and contested questions asked much of a region emerging from conflict. The referendum arguably challenged political leaders in Northern Ireland to discuss these issues before they were ready to do so.

Considered (and contested) contributions: The EU referendum and the Irish government

The Irish government took up the economic and political themes during its contributions to the referendum discussion, but did not stray into any discussion of how a vote for the UK to leave the EU might impact on Ireland's constitutional future. The possibility of Brexit was identified as a "strategic risk" of critical importance for the Irish state (see Department of the Taoiseach 2016). The severity of the risk prompted the Irish government to be active proponents of Remain. Irish government interventions were varied and included speeches, diplomatic activity and visits by leading Irish politicians to the UK and Northern Ireland during the referendum campaign. These high-profile and numerous interventions spoke to a strong Irish preference for the UK to remain in the EU. Irish contributions, however, were not wholly welcomed by unionists, particularly when those contributions suggested that a vote to leave may jeopardize the peace process. DUP Deputy Leader, Nigel Dodds, criticized the then Taoiseach Enda Kenny for such comments (DUP 2016b):

> For politicians outside the United Kingdom to tell us how to vote and lecture us as to what is best for Northern Ireland is disrespectful and will be counterproductive. I trust that Enda

Kenny will keep this in mind when making future comments about the EU referendum.

This was one of the first criticisms of the Irish government's views by the DUP. More followed as the campaign proceeded. DUP unease with the Irish government's pronouncements speaks to broader concerns for the party about the Irish government having a politically motivated interest in influencing the campaign. The Irish government's pro-Remain position placed the Republic of Ireland in the same category as Sinn Féin and the SDLP. The apparent ability of Irish political leaders to infiltrate the referendum campaign smacked of Irish interference in sovereign UK affairs. It alarmed the DUP because it touched on some of the party's deepest fears about a creeping form of Irish nationalism and a united Ireland by stealth.

The EU referendum result in Northern Ireland

The referendum result in Northern Ireland was largely as expected – 55.8 per cent of voters voted Remain. Turnout was relatively low, almost ten percentage points lower than for the UK as a whole, and 8 per cent less than the turnout figure for the Northern Ireland Assembly election a few weeks earlier. A heavy emphasis on the potential economic effects of Brexit by parties during the campaign, however, did not diminish the political edge to the referendum debate and result. In other words, the EU referendum campaign in Northern Ireland did not free voters from their traditional political and constitutional allegiances (Carmichael 2016: 87): "Ultimately, therefore, the majority of the electorate in Northern Ireland behaved largely by reference to the issue which defines politics here, namely, the constitutional question and the border with the Republic of Ireland".

Nationalist and unionist voters heeded the cues from their respective political leaders (Coakley & Garry 2016):

85% of Catholics supported "remain", but only 41% of Protestants did so (with 59% supporting Brexit). There were similar differences in other, overlapping, areas of division: 88% of those describing themselves as Irish supported "remain", but only 38% of those describing themselves as British took this position (with Northern Irish identifiers in between, at 64%). Among those describing themselves as "nationalist", similarly, 89% supported "remain", a position adopted only by 35% who described themselves as unionist (with those opting for "neither" coming in the middle, at 70%).[14]

Nationalists overwhelmingly supported the Remain position. Given the clear and unambiguous cues they received from their political representatives, this high level of support for Remain is unsurprising. Unionists, on the other hand, were more likely to vote Leave.

The referendum outcome in Northern Ireland also demonstrates a clear East–West regional divide and this has political connotations. Eleven of Northern Ireland's 18 constituencies voted Remain, including the Belfast constituencies and all border constituencies. All constituencies represented by a nationalist or independent MP returned a vote in favour of continued EU membership, while three constituencies with unionist representation in Westminster also supported Remain. The remaining seven constituencies that voted Leave are those with unionist majorities and represented by unionist MPs (see Table 2.5).

The referendum result in Northern Ireland is interesting because although political persuasion was broadly an indicator of voter choice, it did not produce evidence of a *stark* communal divide on the question of continued EU membership: "A simplistic nationalist/unionist explanation for the Northern Ireland vote is not convincing" (Mills & Colvin 2016). The cohesion demonstrated by nationalist voters is not apparent for unionism, which did not vote as a strong and united communal bloc, that is over a third of unionists voted Remain.

In the aftermath of the referendum outcome, however, nationalists, and Sinn Féin in particular, railed against the decision, demanding that the will of the Northern Ireland electorate be respected. In contrast, unionists, including the UUP, which had campaigned for Remain, accepted the result as the sovereign decision of the entire UK and has demonstrated clear support for the UK government's moves to take the UK, in its entirety, out of the EU.

---

14. These figures are based on the results of a major survey conducted in the weeks immediately before and after the referendum, and are based on a sample of 4,000. The survey was supported by the UK's Economic and Social Research Council.

Table 2.5 EU referendum result across Northern Ireland constituencies

Constituency	MP representation	Turnout	Leave	Remain
East Antrim	Unionist	65%	55%	45%
East Belfast	Unionist	66%	51%	49%
East Londonderry	Unionist	60%	48%	52%
Fermanagh and South Tyrone	Unionist	68%	41%	59%
Foyle	Nationalist	57%	22%	78%
Lagan Valley	Unionist	66%	53%	47%
Mid Ulster	Nationalist	62%	40%	60%
Newry and Armagh	Nationalist	64%	37%	63%
North Antrim	Unionist	65%	62%	38%
North Belfast	Unionist	57%	49%	51%
North Down	Independent	67%	48%	52%
South Antrim	Unionist	63%	51%	49%
South Belfast	Nationalist	67%	30%	70%
South Down	Nationalist	62%	33%	67%
Strangford	Unionist	64%	55%	45%
Upper Bann	Unionist	64%	53%	47%
West Belfast	Nationalist	49%	26%	74%
West Tyrone	Nationalist	62%	33%	67%

Source: Murphy (2016c).

There is nevertheless discernible levels of unease in Northern Ireland following the EU referendum. Voters have expressed negative feelings about how the region will fare outside the EU. Fifty-three per cent of respondents to the 2016 Northern Ireland Life and Times Survey felt that Northern Ireland would probably or definitely be worse off. Respondents also noted concerns about their own situation – 48 per cent thought they would be worse off in the context of Brexit; 25 per cent gauged that they would be better off; and a sizeable minority of 26 per cent were unsure of their personal situation outside the EU (see Gormley-Heenan *et al.* 2017). The same survey revealed concerns among voters about possible problems crossing the border after UK withdrawal from the EU. Those who cross the border more regularly were more likely to be worried about the border. In a detailed study and survey of the Irish border region and Brexit, Hayward (2017a: 15) found: "The overwhelming sense is one of uncertainty; this is not a good thing in a Border Region with a legacy of conflict and under-development". Ninety-seven per cent of respondents (from both sides of the border) said that they would be personally affected by Brexit while 82 per cent said the impact on them would be significant (Hayward 2017a: 60). Their key concerns centred on how travel between Northern Ireland/ UK and the Republic of Ireland might be impacted by Brexit, and on the anticipated changes for Irish passport holders in the UK/Northern Ireland, and British passport holders in the Republic of Ireland.

It is interesting to note that the number of applications from Northern Ireland for Irish passports has risen considerably since the EU referendum vote. In 2017, there were over 80,000 passport applications from Northern Ireland. This was over 10,000 more applications than was received from Northern Ireland in 2016, and almost 30,000 more applications than the year leading up to the EU referendum (Power 2017). Interest in obtaining an Irish passport is not just discernible among Northern Ireland nationalists. Former UUP MP Danny Kinahan noted that some of his unionist constituents had sought advice from him about how to apply for an Irish passport (*The News Letter*, 29 June 2016). Perhaps even more surprisingly, DUP MP Ian Paisley Jnr advised voters in a tweet: "My advice is if you are entitled to second passport then take one. I sign off lots of applications for constituents" (24 June 2016). By applying for Irish passports, Northern Ireland citizens have been mobilized by Brexit and have acted to offset the potential disruption to free movement on the island of Ireland and across the EU following the UK's exit from the EU.

The EU referendum – both the campaign and the outcome – produced ambiguity and uncertainty in Northern Ireland. The work of the Executive and Assembly was hampered by an unwillingness to confront key political issues. Nationalist political parties were coherent and clear in their support for Remain; unionist parties were variously ambiguous and vague. Reluctant to upset their divided constituencies, civil society was cautious and guarded in its engagement with the referendum campaign. The Brexit vote also exposed a fracture in the previously strong consensus-based approach to Northern Ireland that had become typical of British–Irish cooperation. This upset what had been a hallmark of the peace process. Northern Ireland's "negative peace" and the continuing lack of trust across Northern Ireland politics and society meant that communal tensions were never far from the surface. Politicians, parties, institutions and interest groups acted to keep a lid on potentially destabilizing forces. Additional developments and disagreements, however, many of them unrelated to Brexit, materialized in the months following the referendum and they further antagonized Northern Ireland's tenuous political situation.

Scandal, suspension and more elections: Continuing volatility in Northern Ireland

Following the EU referendum result, there were some tentative signs that both political traditions in Northern Ireland were focused on trying to deal constructively with the outcome. An early example of unity from the Northern Ireland Executive came in the form of a joint letter written by the first minister and deputy first minister to the UK prime minister. The letter outlined key concerns following the UK vote to leave the EU, and it focused on five key issues where Northern Ireland interests might be threatened (see Table 2.6)

The letter requested that the Northern Ireland administration be fully involved and engaged in negotiations between the Irish and UK governments on the question of the border. It also detailed "constructive initial discussions with the Irish government" through the NSMC, and looked forward to further engagement with the prime minister and colleagues. This may be all the more significant because following the 2016 Assembly elections, the Northern Ireland Executive was formed by the DUP and Sinn Féin alone. For the first time, the SDLP and UUP chose to take their seats on the opposition benches and did not participate in the power-sharing Executive. These developments suggested that: "Initial fears that the diametrically opposed views on Brexit of these parties [DUP and Sinn Féin] would destabilize the devolved government proved largely unfounded" (Birrell & Heenan 2017: 476).

This outward initial show of unity, however, masked a significant lingering chasm between the two Executive parties. Within a few months, political arrangements collapsed following a major dispute between Sinn Féin and the DUP about the alleged mismanagement of the Renewable Heat Incentive (RHI) scheme. The scheme offered

Table 2.6 Key Brexit issues for Northern Ireland

Issue	Detail
Status of land border between Northern Ireland and the Republic of Ireland	Border must not become an impediment to the movement of people, goods and services; it must not become a catalyst for illegal activity; and it must not create an incentive for those who would wish to undermine the peace process and political settlement.
Retention of competitiveness	Critical to the Northern Ireland economy that all businesses retain their competitiveness; are not subject to additional costs; and preserve access to labour.
Protection of energy sector	Imperative to avoid undermining the energy sector, which is already subject to cost and supply issues.
Uncertainty around EU funding	Concerns about Northern Ireland's ability to draw down EU funding, and the absence of EU programmes in the future, given the importance of EU funding to the economy and peace process.
Impact on the agri-food sector and fisheries	Worries about the vulnerability of the Northern Ireland agricultural and fisheries sector to the loss of EU receipts from the CAP, and the potential introduction of tariff and non-tariff barriers to trade.

Source: Letter from Northern Ireland first minister and deputy first minister to Prime Minister Theresa May, dated 10 August 2016, available at: https://www.executiveoffice-ni.gov.uk/sites/default/files/publications/execoffice/Letter%20to%20PM%20from%20FM%20%26%20dFM.pdf (accessed 12 March 2018).

non-domestic users a financial incentive to install renewable heat energy systems. However, there were serious systematic failings in the administration of the scheme, which allowed for substantial abuse of the system. A report by the comptroller and auditor general for Northern Ireland (Northern Ireland Audit Office 2016: 115) noted: "This scheme has had serious systemic weaknesses from the start". The spiralling cost of financing the scheme eventually led to its closure owing to the severe financial risk that continued implementation of the initiative posed to Northern Ireland's block grant. First Minister Arlene Foster was the enterprise minister at the time the RHI scheme was rolled out and so was in charge of the department with responsibility for it. She rejected allegations that she had mismanaged the scheme and was steadfast in her refusal to step aside. Sinn Féin was especially vociferous in calling for the first minister to do so. In early January 2017, the late Martin McGuinness resigned as deputy first minister in protest at the DUP's handling of the scandal. This move collapsed the Executive and Sinn Féin's subsequent refusal to enter talks aimed at resolving the crisis precipitated the calling of Assembly elections. The deputy first minister criticized the DUP's "arrogance" and the party's "failure to accept the principles of power sharing and parity of esteem and their handling of the RHI crisis". Sinn Féin, however, was also motivated by other lingering difficulties in the party's relationship with the DUP. In his resignation letter, McGuinness noted (Sinn Féin 2017a):

> The equality, mutual respect and all-Ireland approaches enshrined in the Good Friday Agreement have never been fully embraced by the DUP. Apart from the negative attitude to nationalism and to the Irish identity and culture, there has been a shameful disrespect towards many other sections of our community. Women, the LGBT community and ethnic minorities have all felt this prejudice. And for those who wish to live their lives through the medium of Irish, elements in the DUP have exhibited the most crude and crass bigotry.

Frustration with the DUP's refusal to deal satisfactorily with the Irish language and the past were clearly also a factor in prompting Sinn Féin to go to the electorate. The RHI scandal brought matters to a head, but it was borne out of a persistent lack of trust between Sinn Féin and the DUP around failures to address and resolve outstanding issues. Northern Ireland's "negative peace" meant that the stability of political arrangements was susceptible to any development that highlighted a lack of equality and respect. The RHI scandal and its aftermath further polarized relations between the DUP and Sinn Féin. The collapse of the system represented a low point in the relationship, and set the scene for another bruising electoral encounter.

Shifting electoral arithmetic: The 2017 Northern Ireland Assembly election

The 2017 Northern Ireland Assembly election was another largely pre-dictable electoral contest. The DUP maintained their position as the largest party with Sinn Féin in second place (see Table 2.7). The overall election outcome, however, masks some very interesting shifts in voting preferences and patterns. The most striking outcome of the 2017 Assembly election is the increase in support for Sinn Féin. The party won 27 seats, its largest ever share of Assembly seats and just one seat less than the DUP. The SDLP scored 12 Assembly seats. The combined nationalist tally meant that nationalists had 39 of the Assembly's 90 seats.[15] Nationalist candidates benefited from an increased electoral turnout, and significantly, non-unionist voters voted in greater numbers than unionists. On the unionist side of the house, the DUP maintained its status as the largest political party in the Northern Ireland Assembly. However, the 2017 Assembly election was a disappointing one as the party shed ten seats. Even after taking into account the reduced number of Assembly seats, the combined total seat tally for all unionist parties was 40, just one seat more than their nationalist counterparts. Perhaps more significantly however, this was the first time that the unionist outright majority had been undermined. Unionist political parties no longer dominated in Northern Ireland.

Table 2.7 Northern Ireland Assembly election results 2017

Party	Seats	Vote share	+/- %
DUP	28	28.1%	-1.1
Sinn Féin	27	27.9%	+3.9
SDLP	12	11.9%	-0.1
UUP	10	12.9%	+0.3
APNI	8	9.1%	+2.1
Green Party	2	2.3%	-0.4
TUV	1	2.6%	-0.9
PBPA	1	1.8%	-0.2
Independents	1	1.8%	-1.5

---

15. The Stormont House Agreement (2014) included a commitment to reduce the number of Northern Ireland MLAs. This meant that the 2017 Assembly election would elect a 90-member Assembly, as compared with the 108-member Assembly elected in 2016. This was achieved by Northern Ireland's 18 constituencies going from being six to five member constituencies.

Middle-ground political parties did relatively well. The APNI had a very good election. The party held onto all of its eight seats, despite the overall reduction in the size of the Assembly. Similarly, the Green Party retained its two seats. On the outer edges of the party system, the TUV maintained its single Assembly seat and the PBPA went from having two seats to one seat. There was some evidence too of cross-community voting. Some successful nationalist SDLP candidates owe their victories to vote transfers from the smaller, moderate UUP.

The 2017 Assembly election campaign was little different to previous campaigns. "Bread and butter" policy issues did receive some limited airing, but traditional political rivalries tended to dominate electoral discourse. The DUP's manifesto had a defensive character (DUP 2017: 7):

> While we will not be prepared to give in to radical republican demands there is a danger that the government in the face of an election victory by Sinn Féin would be prepared to make compromises on the basis of the mandate they have won. This must not be allowed to happen.

The party focused more on strategy than policy. It detailed ten principles that would govern the DUP's approach to post-election negotiations aimed at forming a new Executive. These were not policy-focused, instead they were about challenging Sinn Féin and protecting unionist interests. The politics of old – nationalist versus unionist – remained apparent, and there was little in the way of the politics of reconciliation.

Sinn Féin's campaign messaging was focused on calls for "equality, integrity and respect". The party manifesto was particularly critical of the DUP, which, according to Sinn Féin, "has refused to adhere to the principles of the Good Friday Agreement, equality of treatment, parity of esteem and mutual respect for all citizens" (Sinn Féin 2017b: 8). The contents of the manifesto considered a range of political issues including: "integrity in government" (a direct reference to the DUP's handling of the RHI scandal); "equality and respect" (including calls for an Irish language act and marriage equality, both of which the DUP oppose); a "united Ireland"; and "engaging with the legacy of the past". All of these were contested issues that exposed a clear unionist–nationalist divide. They represented outstanding issues that unionists and nationalists had failed to address during the latter stages of the peace process. The remnants of the conflict continued to find expression in contemporary Northern Ireland electoral contests and continued to infect political and communal relations thus limiting the potential for Northern Ireland to constructively address other current policy challenges, few of which are as potentially destabilizing as Brexit. Both party manifestos considered the Brexit vote, but expressed differing views on how to meet the challenge. Sinn Féin rehearsed its commitment to work for "special designated status for Northern Ireland" (discussed further in Chapters 4 and 5) while the DUP wished to see the referendum result upheld. The election did not lead to the immediate resurrection of the Northern Ireland devolved institutions. The DUP and Sinn Féin remained locked in a stand-off about terms for reinstating the power-sharing arrangement. During this protracted and difficult negotiation period, Prime Minister Theresa May triggered Article 50 and formally commenced the process of the UK exiting the EU. This was shortly followed by a surprise general election announcement.

A shock election and startling outcome: The 2017 Westminster election

The prime minister's decision to go to the electorate in June 2017 in an attempt to shore up support for her Brexit negotiating strategy proved to be an extraordinary political misjudgement. The Conservative Party suffered unexpected electoral damage, which resulted in the loss of its majority position in the House of Commons.

From a Northern Ireland perspective, the decision by the prime minister to call a general election demonstrated a distinct lack of regard for the serious political difficulties being encountered there. A further electoral outing disrupted the political talks process in Northern Ireland and sent the parties back into another antagonistic election cycle at a time when relations between the parties were already severely strained. DUP losses and Sinn Féin gains in the earlier Assembly election produced an electoral campaign where parties were highly motivated either to recover lost electoral ground or to capitalize on previous advances. This set the scene for an even more hostile election. The prime minister evidently had little regard for how an election conducted in such an atmosphere might halt, even roll back progress in Northern Ireland. This level of British detachment from (and ignorance of) Northern

Ireland's political difficulties signalled a pronounced challenge to the delicately balanced unionist–nationalist equilibrium.

The Westminster election in Northern Ireland recorded a turnout of 65.6 per cent, the highest turnout for a Westminster election since 2005. Sinn Féin repeated their electoral gains and secured three additional Westminster seats. But it was also a good election for the DUP, which returned ten MPs, an increase of two since 2015. The main casualties were the moderate unionist and nationalist parties, the UUP and SDLP. Both parties lost all of their seats, which were won by their less moderate unionist and nationalist party opponents (see Table 2.8). The election result suggested that the polarization process had intensified as voters identified with those parties adopting hard-line political (and constitutional) positions.

This was not the only surprising feature of the 2017 Westminster election in Northern Ireland. The Conservative Party's poor electoral showing meant that they required a coalition partner. The prime minister was forced to seek out political bedfellows in an attempt to secure her position and that of her party. The post-election composition of the parliament's membership meant the she had little choice but to seek support from the DUP. The party's ten MPs would be sufficient to shore up a majority position for a Conservative Party minority government. Agreement on a confidence-and-supply agreement with the DUP was neither swift nor straightforward. It was agreed almost three weeks after the election, during which time the DUP bargained hard, and

Table 2.8 Northern Ireland Westminster election results 2017

Party	Seats	Vote share	+/- %
DUP	10 (+2)	36.0%	+10.3
Sinn Féin	7 (+3)	29.4%	+4.9
SDLP	0 (-3)	11.7%	-2.2
UUP	0 (-2)	10.3%	-5.8
APNI	0	7.9%	-0.6
Green Party	0	0.9%	0.0
TUV	0	0.4%	-1.9
Independents	1	3.3%	-1.8

eventually came away with £1 billion in new funding for Northern Ireland. The funding was earmarked to support several initiatives including infrastructure projects, health service improvements and the provision of ultra-fast broadband, and clearly the additional financial support benefits all the people of Northern Ireland. The non-financial component of the agreement required the DUP to support the Conservative Party on key votes. These included, for example, the Queen's Speech, budget and Brexit. The DUP strategy in terms of reaching agreement with the Conservative Party was resolutely focused on securing a financial package for Northern Ireland. The DUP's approach to the negotiation with the Conservative Party saw the party "keep its focus economic, its price high and the rewards ongoing, via a regular review of the arrangement" (Tonge 2017a: 416). There were other policy stipulations in terms of maintaining the status quo on pensions and the winter fuel allowance, but otherwise the agreement between the DUP and Conservative Party had a clear financial focus. The sole reference to Brexit in the document commits the DUP to support the government on legislation pertaining to the UK exit from the EU (*Agreement between the Conservative and Unionist Party and the Democratic Unionist Party on Support for the Government in Parliament* 2017: 1). The agreement contains no further detail on Brexit. The DUP did not see the negotiations with the Conservative Party as presenting an opportunity to influence the overall UK approach to Brexit. There was no push from the DUP for the Conservative Party to pursue a soft Brexit in terms of staying in the single market or customs union, even though such an outcome would help to satisfy the DUP's desire for there to be no hard border on the island of Ireland. Sources close to the negotiators suggest that the DUP was content to leave the Brexit issue to central government. The party had faith in the ability of the centre to manage Brexit on behalf of the entire UK.

The DUP–Conservative Party deal was met with much disapproval from within Northern Ireland, but also across the UK. Other parties in Northern Ireland were concerned at the appropriateness of an arrangement that gave the DUP political leverage over the British government. This led to questions about the impartiality of the British government in its dealings with Northern Ireland, and particularly during periods of crisis. The arrangement also altered the traditional basis for British–Irish engagement on the Northern Ireland issue in that the British government was now closely connected (and dependent on) the largest unionist party in Northern Ireland. The Irish government conveyed to Prime Minister Theresa May that the deal should not put the Belfast Agreement at risk. Wider objections to the DUP were linked to the right-wing social conservatism of the party, and specifically the party's opposition to marriage equality and abortion.[16] Where Northern Ireland/Ireland was an afterthought in the context of the EU referendum, the post-referendum landscape places Northern Ireland at the heart of UK politics during the Brexit negotiation period.

The politicization of Brexit in Northern Ireland

De Wilde *et al.* (2016: 3) conceptualize politicization as "a three-dimensional process involving increasing salience, polarization of opinion and the expansion of actors and audiences involved in EU issues". Northern Ireland's "negative peace" environment was receptive to the kinds of forces that Brexit unleashed. The EU referendum, the elections and the various, sometimes unexpected, related developments produced a series of forces that tally with the components and manifestations of politicization. At all three levels in Northern Ireland – the micro, meso and macro – empirical and anecdotal evidence points to the increased salience of the EU; greater contestation and polarization of parties, groups and individuals; and an expansion in the number and diversity of actors mobilized by the Brexit question. De Wilde *et al.* (2016: 4) offer a neat means of documenting and measuring the extent to which politicization can be detected:

> Most students of politicisation refer to a component of importance (societal actors consider EU issues more important for their interests or values), a behavioural component (societal actors spend more resources on contesting or influencing EU issues), a preference component (opinions diverge about what the EU should be and do) and a socialisation component (more societal actors become attentive and/or engaged in EU affairs).

---

16. These issues were not part of the confidence-and-supply agreement.

Societal actors and citizens in Northern Ireland have become more attuned to the EU and to the consequences of the EU referendum vote for many aspects of their lives. This is found most emphatically among citizens around the border area (see Hayward 2017a) but concerns about Brexit have also been expressed by political parties and civil society in Northern Ireland. Northern Ireland's political institutions have been relatively quiet; not all interest groups have taken a position on Brexit; and the number of new contributors to the debate is small. In these cases, difference exists but it has not been overtly expressed. However, the analysis suggests a reluctance to discuss Brexit for the very fact that it exposes polarized views. To some extent, this is understandable, and maybe welcome given the potential for disagreement that such conversations might produce when set against a "negative peace" backdrop.

In behavioural terms, societal actors have spent more resources on contesting certain preferences. Political parties have produced manifesto promises and policy documents. Interest groups, including the UFU and CBI, have published analyses of the impact of Brexit for their sectors. Greater academic interest has been substantially evident. The Irish government has been particularly active in seeking to influence the EU and the UK. Substantial resources have been committed to arguing the Irish government's position at various levels and in a variety of settings (discussed further in Chapter 4).

There is clear evidence too of diverging opinions on Brexit in Northern Ireland. This was evident during the EU referendum campaign but became more emphatic following the result. The preferences of nationalists and unionists are different. Their interpretation of what UK withdrawal from the EU means differ, as do their formulations about Northern Ireland's status outside the EU (this is discussed in greater detail in Chapter 5). The interplay between domestic issues including the RHI scandal, the Irish language act and marriage equality also polarized parties and voters during this period.

The politicization of the EU and Brexit is evident in Northern Ireland and Brexit has produced a polarizing effect. The extent to which politicization has been empowering or limiting is considered in future chapters. Hard economic reality may be the catalyst that compels Northern Ireland's political and civic leaders to overcome the polarizing effect of Brexit. Despite differences across the communal divide, there is a shared understanding that Brexit is problematic for Northern Ireland.

Many of these problems have an economic character. The next chapter examines the extent to which Northern Ireland will be economically affected by the UK decision to leave the EU. It points to the interplay between economics and politics in a divided society where Brexit threatens economic and political gains, achieved in the context of the peace process, and introduces an atmosphere of political and constitutional uncertainty.

3

When introverted politics and political economy collide

The Northern Ireland conflict and related political difficulties are well-known and well documented. The most immediate and visible impact has been in terms of lives lost, injuries sustained and hardship endured. The Troubles, however, reached into every facet and dimension of Northern Ireland society, and the local economy in particular was a serious casualty. Economic decline during the Troubles contrasts with the early years after the partition of the island of Ireland, when the Northern Ireland economy was strong (Rowthorn 1981: 3): "When Northern Ireland was created [in 1920] it was seen as an integral and self-supporting component of Britain's imperial system, able to generate a surplus and help finance the military and other expenses involved in running the Empire."

Agriculture, ship-building and a thriving linen industry were the backbone of Northern Ireland's indigenous industrial base. However, the downturn in the manufacturing industry from the 1970s onwards hit Northern Ireland's home-grown industries badly. The economic decline that followed also coincided with the onset of the conflict. During the 1970s and 1980s, the regional economy was in the doldrums. Against the backdrop of violence and serious political instability, foreign investment dried up, manufacturing stalled, outward migration grew and growth halted. Northern Ireland's focus on local arguments was producing an introverted form of politics that was seriously undermining its economic well-being.

For a sustained period during the Troubles, the Northern Ireland economy lagged behind the rest of the UK and has persistently been the poorest performing of the UK's 12 regions. From the 1990s onwards, the achievement of the peace process and the signing of the Belfast Agreement signalled a turning point in Northern Ireland's economic fortunes. Since the 2000s, the so-called "peace dividend" may not have fully materialized (see Coulter 2014; O'hearn 2008), but nevertheless economic opportunities that presented themselves in the context of the peace process were an important factor in rejuvenating the Northern Ireland economy. In particular, inward investment increased, and there was also some growth in the construction, tourism and services sectors. The global economic crisis did dent the region's longer-term recovery, and crucially, persistent structural problems continue to beset the Northern Ireland economy.

The impact of the "peace dividend" may be disputed, but a more subtle shift in Northern Ireland's economic fortunes can be traced to the early years of the peace process, a period that coincides with the completion of the single European market (SEM). There was an important symbolic context to SEM membership for Northern Ireland. By eradicating trade borders on the island of Ireland, the single market brought not just economic advantages, but political benefits too, particularly for nationalists. Northern Ireland's traditionally distant relationship with the EU began to alter as the region slowly embraced the new opportunities associated with the completion of the SEM, the doubling of the EU structural funds in 1988, and the creation of the Peace and Reconciliation Fund in 1995. Collectively, these developments became agencies of change in the political economy of all of Ireland. This was clearly aided by the evolving peace process, which created an environment more amenable to economic growth and development. Institutional linkages between Northern Ireland and the Republic of Ireland further cemented economic relationships on the island. In their totality, these developments tacitly facilitated a degree of all-island economic cooperation that has been to the benefit of both Northern Ireland and the Republic of Ireland, and that has strengthened consistently over time. These positive economic developments and achievements were important factors in helping to stabilize and grow the Northern Ireland economy. The economic spoils, however, have not been extensive and nor were they evenly shared across Northern Ireland society. Persistent and growing inequality has been part and parcel of the region's recent economic experience.

In EU terms, Northern Ireland is classified as one of the NUTS 2 transition regions. This categorization means that its GDP per inhabitant is between 75 and 90 per cent of the EU average. Northern Ireland has benefited from EU financial support, although this has never been comparable in size or significance to the annual block grant from Westminster. The region continues to be heavily reliant on funding from the UK Treasury, supports a comparatively large public service, and still suffers from having lost much of its traditional industrial and manufacturing base. All of these factors make the Northern Ireland economy something of a peculiarity. It has been variously described as "complex and intriguing" (Budd 2017: 113) and "lamentable" (*The Economist*, 22 January 2015).

Northern Ireland's economy has encountered some structural and performance related changes. These have been influenced by a selection of developments including the peace process, the SEM/EU, economic crisis and now Brexit. The most profound of these is likely to be the UK withdrawal from the EU, a development that starkly threatens the economic gains and relationships that have been achieved in recent years in Northern Ireland. The absence of clarity about what precisely Brexit means and its anticipated impact over time heightens economic uncertainty. The situation has been further exacerbated by political instability, and in particular, by the suspension of the Northern Ireland institutions. This has interrupted devolved politics and undermined the regional policy agenda that can support economic development and forward planning. This chapter documents the threats to the Northern Ireland economy arising from Brexit and details how these interplay, in sometimes troubling ways, with forces for political and constitutional change.

Recent economic performance in Northern Ireland

Since the EU referendum vote in June 2016, and despite some dire predictions, the performance of the Northern Ireland economy has remained stable. The Northern Ireland growth rate was 1.6 per cent in 2015 and 1.4 per cent in 2016 (PWC 2017: 3). A weaker sterling helped to boost Northern Ireland exports, which were 11.7 per cent higher in 2016 than in 2015 (Danske Bank 2017: 1). Strong economic recovery in the Republic of Ireland, an important trading partner, is also likely to have been a factor in supporting economic stability immediately after the Brexit vote. There are nevertheless some signs that the impact of Brexit is beginning to be felt in Northern Ireland. In broad terms, Northern Ireland's future economic prospects are not predicted to be strong.

Inflation increased by 0.47 percentage points more than the UK average in Northern Ireland and this is linked to the Brexit vote (Breinlich *et al.* 2017: 13). This is because Northern Ireland households spend relatively more on high import share products and relatively less on low import shares. Economic growth forecasts were also revised downwards. Growth is set to continue but at a slower pace (see Table 3.1). Northern Ireland's estimated growth levels are also below what is predicted for the UK as a whole, with growth there predicted to be 1.4 per cent in 2017 and 1.5 per cent in 2018. The contrast with the Republic of Ireland is even more stark, where growth levels are predicted to be between 3.2 per cent and 3.6 per cent in 2017 and 2018 (see PWC 2017: 3).

Northern Ireland's slow growth rate means that GVA per capita is among the lowest in the UK. The gap between UK GVA per capita and Northern Ireland GVA per capita actually grew by 2.75 times between 1997 and 2014 (Northern Ireland Assembly Research and Information Service 2016b: 4).

A key factor that impacts on Northern Ireland's long-term economic performance is unemployment rates, which reached their lowest level in nine years in mid-2017 when the unemployment figure fell to 4 per cent and dipped below the UK figure for the first time since 2013 (see Northern Ireland Statistics and Research Agency (NISRA) 2017a: 8). The Northern Ireland unemployment figure is also lower than the unemployment rate in the Republic of Ireland and lower than the EU average (see Table 3.2). Long-term unemployment in Northern Ireland, however, is consistently high: 51 per cent of total unemployment in 2016 (Northern Ireland Assembly Research and Information Service 2016b: 5). Moreover, analysts predict that unemployment in Northern Ireland will rise marginally from 2018 (Danske Bank 2017: 4).

Table 3.1 Estimated Northern Ireland growth levels

Year	PWC*	EY**	Danske Bank***
2017	1.0%	1.1%	1.2%
2018	0.9%	0.8%	1.0%

* PWC (2017).

** EY (2017). Note: The EY economic forecast does predict that Northern Ireland growth will increase to 1.4 per cent by 2020.

*** Danske Bank (2017).

Table 3.2 Unemployment rates for EU28, UK, Republic of Ireland and Northern Ireland 2006–16

	2006	2007	2008	2009	2010	2011	2012	2013	2014	2015	2016
EU28	8.2	7.2	7.0	9.0	9.6	9.7	10.5	10.9	10.2	9.4	8.5
UK	5.4	5.3	5.6	7.6	7.8	8.1	7.9	7.6	6.1	5.3	4.8
Northern Ireland	4.4	3.9	4.4	6.4	7.1	7.2	7.4	7.5	6.4	6.1	5.7
Ireland	4.5	4.7	6.4	12.0	13.9	14.7	14.7	13.1	11.3	9.4	7.9

Source: EU28, UK and Republic of Ireland figures from *Eurostat Statistics*, available at: http://ec.europa.eu/eurostat/statistics-explained/index. php/File:Unemployment_rate_2005-2016_(%25)_new.png. Northern Ireland figures from *Eurostat (Regions and Cities)*, available at: http:// ec.europa.eu/eurostat/cache/RCI/#?vis=nuts2.labourmarket&lang=en.

Relatively low unemployment figures for Northern Ireland, however, mask other problematic features of the region's employment picture, namely high economic inactivity rates compared to the rest of the UK and low productivity rates, which are consistently below the national average and are a sector-wide problem: "Northern Ireland is a low productivity region, within a country that performs poorly against comparator economies" (Northern Ireland Assembly Research and Information Service 2016b: 7).

Other persistent structural problems in Northern Ireland include an over-reliance on public sector employment and an under-developed private sector. In 2017, approximately 27 per cent of the Northern Ireland workforce was employed in the public sector (NISRA 2017b: 21). The equivalent figure for the UK as a whole was 17 per cent (Office for National Statistics (ONS) 2017: 3). Public spending per head in Northern Ireland is also higher than for any other part of the UK and stands at 21 per cent above the UK average (Keep & Brien 2017: 3). The explanation for such a significant differential between the rest of the UK and Northern Ireland can be linked to legacy and security issues related to the Northern Ireland conflict, and is also connected to the diseconomies of scale that attach to governing a small population. Importantly however: "The figures do not support the notion that public sector employment is crowding out the private sector, rather that there is a structural weakness within the Northern Ireland private sector" (Mac Flynn 2015: 2). The seriousness of this structural problem has long been recognized and attempts to rebalance the economy have consistently formed part of successive Northern Ireland agreements, Programmes for Government and economic initiatives.

Rebalancing and rebuilding the Northern Ireland economy: Proposals and problems

A strong emphasis on increasing Northern Ireland's economic competitiveness by growing and bolstering the private sector has been a central feature of various government proposals. In the context of supporting and buttressing Northern Ireland's post-conflict society, there has been a strong emphasis on ensuring not just political, but also economic stability. In practice, this has meant addressing the peculiarities of the Northern Ireland economy in order to allow the region to reap the economic benefits associated with peace. This objective has been central to the work of the devolved institutions. The 1998 Belfast Agreement contained an explicit commitment to economic development in Northern Ireland and bound the British government to making rapid progress on (Belfast Agreement 1998: 20): "a new economic development strategy for Northern Ireland, for consideration in due course by the Assembly, which would provide for short and medium term economic planning linked as appropriate to the regional development strategy".

Later agreements, including the St Andrews Agreement (2006), included additional financial resources to support the policing and justice sector. The Hillsborough Agreement (2010, Annex C) committed both the Irish and UK governments:

> to ensuring the Executive has the capacity to provide quality public services, to continue the process of necessary reform, to plan for the future, to make the long-term capital investments to underpin the economic transformation of Northern Ireland, as well as bringing long-term benefits for the island as a whole.

Whereas the above agreements were concerned predominantly with the policing and justice sector, the Stormont House Agreement (2014) is more explicitly focused on addressing some of the Northern Ireland economy's persistent structural difficulties. A £2 billion package aimed to support a comprehensive programme of public sector reform and restructuring and included measures to address structural differences in relation to the cost of managing a divided society. This involved the extension of shared services and a reduction in the size and cost of the Northern Ireland civil service and the wider public sector (Stormont House Agreement 2014: 1). The Agreement also contained a commitment to introduce legislation to enable the devolution of corporation tax in 2017.[1]

---

1. The suspension of devolution in Northern Ireland in early 2017 interrupted the roll-out of a reduced corporation tax rate of 12.5 per cent in Northern Ireland. The proposed new and lower rate matches the corporation tax rate that applies in the Republic of Ireland. Lowering the Northern Ireland corporation tax rate will result in the loss of £500–700 million per annum in budgetary transfers from the UK government under the Barnett formula. The utility of this tool however, is undermined by Brexit (Budd 2017: 121): "Without access to the SEM and/or remaining in the EU's customs union, the logic of harmonized CT [corporation tax] rates with the ROI [Republic of Ireland] is undermined as the transaction costs of FDI [foreign direct investment] locating in NI [Northern Ireland] increase significantly."

The Northern Ireland Executive was also proactive in attempting to confront economic challenges in Northern Ireland. The draft *Programme for Government 2016–2021* was constructed using an outcomes-based approach. The first and over-riding outcome priority is: "We prosper through a strong, competitive regionally balanced economy" (Northern Ireland Executive 2016: 12). The key indicators for achieving this outcome included private sector NICEI (Northern Ireland Composite Economic Index), external sales, rate of innovation activity and employment rate by council area. An emphasis on improving the competitiveness of the Northern Ireland economy was also evident in the region's *Economic Strategy* (Northern Ireland Executive 2012: 9), which set out the Executive's economic vision for 2030: "An economy characterized by a sustainable and growing private sector, where a greater number of firms compete in global markets and there is growing employment and prosperity for all". The strategy aimed to respond to the volatile global economy during the period after the economic crisis, and it prioritized the twin objectives of rebalancing and rebuilding the Northern Ireland economy.

The *Investment Strategy for Northern Ireland 2011–2021* involves a multi-billion pound financial stimulus to support economic recovery and growth. The strategy is focused on capital investment and the creation of a modern and efficient infrastructure, and it also formed part of the Northern Ireland Executive's commitment "to encourage cohesion, sharing and integration at all levels to build a united community" (Northern Ireland Executive 2015: 7). The 2017 DUP–Conservative Party confidence-and-supply agreement included a financial package that also aimed to stimulate private sector activity through, for example, investment in ultrafast broadband and infrastructure.

Devolution has allowed the political institutions in Northern Ireland to consider ways and means of addressing the region's structural economic problems and weak competitiveness. There are, however, mixed views about the extent to which political decentralization can produce economic dividends (see Brownlow 2017). A key obstacle here is the institutional geography of the asymmetrical UK devolution settlement, which to date has not proved effective in addressing persistent spatial imbalances across the UK. There is a persuasive case here for the mechanics of the devolved fiscal arrangement to be altered to allow for underlying structural conditions to be addressed more robustly by devolved authorities. The standard approach to date in Northern Ireland has been for the devolved authorities to seek financial stimulus packages and more recently, to push for the devolution of corporation tax. Birnie and Brownlow (2017) are reticent about the ability of a reduced corporation tax rate to address Northern Ireland's structural economic problems. Instead they note that boosting competitiveness and addressing longstanding regional distortions is the primary means to achieve economic gains and to ensure the long-term health of the Northern Ireland economy. Electioneering and the suspension of the devolved institutions, however, has meant that there has been limited opportunity for the Northern Ireland Assembly or Executive to pursue or implement key economic objectives including public spending reforms, economic stimulus packages and a Northern Ireland budget since the Brexit vote in June 2016. Domestic political difficulties meant that the Northern Ireland economy was ill-prepared to meet not just long-term economic challenges, but also the more profound and far-reaching challenges that a UK exit from the EU entails.

The economic implications of Brexit for Northern Ireland: Many negatives, few positives

Analyses of the impact of Brexit point to a range of consequences across different states, settings and sectors. There is a strong consensus that Brexit will have negative implications for the UK. Depending on the type of exit, the UK is calculated to experience a loss of GDP of between 1.31 and 4.21 per cent to 2030 (European Parliament 2017: 29). The effects of Brexit are likely to be felt in the loss of trade and foreign direct investment (FDI), lower productivity and reduced GDP per capita. HM Treasury's analysis of Brexit also depicts a gloomy scenario for each of the three post-Brexit models it analyses for arrangements with the EU, namely European Economic Area (EEA) membership,[2] negotiated bilateral agreement

---

2. The EEA incorporates the four freedoms of the SEM (free movement of goods, people, services and capital) and related policies. EEA members are outside the customs union and the jurisdiction of the European Court of Justice. A study by Doherty *et al.* (2017: 5) notes: "With the EEA, the economic situation and trading environment that EU membership has delivered would remain substantially unchanged, allowing much of the status quo regarding the single market to be maintained … The legal framework, however, would change fundamentally."

and World Trade Organization (HM Government 2016). A negative impact on GDP is predicted to lead to weaker tax receipts, increases in government borrowing and debt, and tax rises or public spending cuts. An OECD study of the impact of Brexit produces similar findings and notes that fiscal savings from stopping net transfers to the EU are likely to have a relatively small impact on UK GDP. The study portrays Brexit as "a major negative shock to the UK economy" (2016: 5). Other studies are similarly pessimistic in their analysis of the impact of Brexit on the UK's economic outlook. Oxford Economics (2016) finds that "most scenarios would impose a significant long-term cost on the UK economy". Dhingra *et al.* (2016) conclude that Brexit will make the UK significantly poorer. A report for Open Europe by Booth *et al.* (2015) is one of the least pessimistic about the impact of Brexit, but even this analysis is dependent on the UK striking a free trade agreement with the EU.

At the level of the EU, the impact of Brexit will not be substantial and is unlikely to be felt at the EU27 macroeconomic level. However, the overall effect of Brexit for the EU27 masks potentially severe differential outcomes for some member states. The Republic of Ireland is expected to suffer the most damaging consequences, and possibly the same magnitude of losses as the UK (European Parliament 2017: 32). An early analysis by the Economic and Social Research Institute (ESRI) identified potentially far-reaching implications for Ireland, particularly in relation to trade and migration (see Barrett *et al.* 2015).

The macroeconomic impact of Brexit on Northern Ireland

The impact of Brexit will be felt differentially across the UK. Northern Ireland, as one of the UK's poorer regions, is expected to experience the most severe consequences (see Springford 2015). In that context, Brexit has the potential to weaken further an already structurally fragile Northern Ireland economy (Soares 2016: 841). The effects will be felt at the macroeconomic level. A briefing note prepared for the Northern Ireland Assembly's Enterprise Committee estimates that economic output in Northern Ireland may fall by 3 per cent when the UK leaves the EU (see Budd 2015). A similar finding emerges from a modelling exercise by Oxford Economics (2016), which indicates that on average by 2030, Northern Ireland's GVA may be 2.8 per cent lower (the figure for the UK as a whole is 1.8 per cent lower).

A key challenge for the Northern Ireland economy in the context of Brexit relates to the region's future trading relationships with the rest of the EU. Northern Ireland has a high degree of trade openness and so international trade is particularly important to the region's economic well-being. This pattern of international trade, however, is based on a comparatively high reliance on trade with the Republic of Ireland. Although the EU is Northern Ireland's largest export market (52 per cent of Northern Ireland exports go to the EU), this includes 38 per cent of Northern Ireland exports that go to the Republic of Ireland (House of Lords 2016: 13). In 2016, goods exports to the Republic of Ireland were valued at £2.4 billion (Northern Ireland Assembly 2017). Trade between the two parts of the island has increased owing to common membership of the SEM, although the volume of trade going from Northern Ireland to the Republic of Ireland is higher than it is in the opposite direction. A 2015 ESRI report notes: "Overall Ireland is more important to Northern Irish exporters than Northern Ireland is for Irish exporters" (Barrett *et al.* 2015: 5) If the UK is to be outside the single market and customs union post-Brexit, the installation of barriers to trade would disrupt cross-border trade. Associated administrative and financial costs would mean an increase in the transaction costs for trading on the island of Ireland, and would lead to a reduction in the volume of North–South and South–North trade. This scenario would impact negatively on Northern Ireland's trading relationship with the Republic of Ireland, and both economies would be subject to severe economic consequences. The significance of Brexit must also be understood in the context of the UK being the most significant market for businesses in Northern Ireland: "sales to Great Britain were worth one and a half times the value of all Northern Ireland exports and nearly four times the value of exports to Ireland in 2015" (HM Government 2017a, Annex). Importantly however, these sales rely on cross-border trade in raw materials and components within complex and integrated supply chains.

A reduction in trade openness would impact differently on specific sectors. Oxford Economics (2016: 7) finds that the two most vulnerable sectors in Northern Ireland would be the construction sector, which would experience a 4.9 per cent contraction, and the manufacturing sector, which would encounter a contraction of 4.1 per cent. There are also concerns about the impact of Brexit on the agri-food sector, which is proportionately more important to the Northern Ireland economy than it is for other parts of the UK. 5.5 per cent of people in Northern Ireland are employed in the agri-food sector, a figure that equates to about 75,000 jobs generating approximately 3.2 per cent of Northern Ireland's GVA (see PWC 2017: 6). The agri-food sector on the island of Ireland is also highly integrated (Irish Farmers' Association (IFA) 2017: 2): "every year thousands of animals and huge volumes of agricultural produce cross the border with Northern Ireland for further finishing or for processing, as part of a complex supply chain".

Under the existing SEM regime, animals and agri-food products often criss-cross the Irish border several times during the processing and packaging stages without being subject to tariffs, checks or obstacles. This entire system of food production and economic activity is fundamentally challenged by Brexit.

The viability of the Northern Ireland agri-food sector is strongly dependent on the EU. Northern Ireland farmers have a heavy reliance on the CAP – 87 per cent of farm income comes from Single Farm Payments, and EU rural development programmes also support a range of projects (House of Lords 2016: 14). Following the EU referendum, the devaluation of sterling against the euro resulted in benefits for Northern Ireland farmers and the agri-food sector, although this rise in prices is not sustainable. The future of Northern Ireland's agri-food sector is precarious. It is vulnerable to changes in the trading relationship between the UK and the EU, and also reliant on a new (and as yet unknown) UK agricultural policy that may or may not reflect current arrangements.

Northern Ireland has a strong record in terms of attracting FDI. Being within the EU has facilitated the region as a site for FDI because membership of the bloc guarantees access to a market of over 500 million consumers. Trade openness is an important determinant in terms of attracting FDI, so when barriers to trade are erected this tends to impact negatively on a region's ability to sustain and promote inward investment. Brexit may trigger a redirecting of inward investment to other parts of the EU (Mac Flynn 2016: 26): "An exit from the EU could deprive Northern Ireland of inward investment by boosting the attractiveness of the Republic of Ireland as a location and reinforcing the peripheral position of Northern Ireland within the UK". Where the UK removal from the EU entails such an impact, this would conflict with the Northern

Ireland Executive's Economic Strategy, which seeks to increase FDI to Northern Ireland (see Northern Ireland Executive 2012).

The impact of Brexit on the Northern Ireland labour market

Related to the impact on trade and FDI is what Brexit will mean for the Northern Ireland labour market. Access to labour is essential to the functioning of the Northern Ireland economy, particularly given that outward migration from the region limits the pool of available talent and labour. Some sectors in Northern Ireland are heavily reliant on non-UK nationals. In the agri-food sector, 60 per cent of factory workers and 90 per cent of seasonal labourers were from outside the UK (House of Lords 2016: 14). On the island of Ireland, the Centre for Cross Border Studies (2016: 8) estimates that 23,000–30,000 people are cross-border workers. The possible introduction of border controls may hinder cross-border commuters and remove some of the EU rights available to workers. A reduction in the availability of labour will have adverse effects for Northern Ireland industries that are heavily dependent on non-UK labour. In a worst case scenario, some of those businesses may choose to relocate south of the border.

Labour market mobility is also reliant on the continuation of the Common Travel Area (CTA) between the UK and the Republic of Ireland. The CTA allows Irish and UK citizens to live, work, study in either jurisdiction. It also entitles Irish citizens to access certain welfare benefits and to vote and stand for election in the UK. This means, for example, that Irish nationals have more rights than other EEA/EU nationals living in the UK. The arrangement means that Irish and UK citizens enjoy special legal status in each other's jurisdiction and this pre-dates EU membership (by several decades). The CTA is particularly important in terms of the lives of Irish citizens living in the UK, and vice versa. It is also important for those on either side of the Irish land border who move easily and unimpeded across that border (often on a daily basis) for the purposes of education, work, healthcare and so on. The CTA facilitates the unfettered mobility of people, and this underpins economic activity. The first phase of the Brexit negotiations between the UK and the EU suggest that the CTA will continue to operate. Its economic significance, coupled with its political and symbolic value, have shielded it from being dismantled.

Brexit and the all-island economy

A further dimension to Brexit is its impact on the all-island economy. InterTradeIreland is responsible for the promotion of an all-island economy. The body "support[s] businesses, through innovation and trade initiatives to take advantage of North/South cooperative opportunities to improve capability, drive competitiveness, growth and jobs". The evolution of InterTradeIreland has been interesting. The body is one of the North–South Implementation Bodies created by the 1998 Belfast Agreement. Designed to coordinate work on trade and business development in areas of mutual interest for the administrations in Northern Ireland and the Republic of Ireland, InterTradeIreland has developed into an effective instrument for all-island business and trade development (Gough & Magennis 2009: 5):

> The body has moved from its political origins in the eyes of business to one that has an economic credibility. There has also been a shift in policy making from taking a regional cross-border view to an all-island one. And finally, a shift from a focus solely on trade to the wider issues of competitiveness.

The development of an-island economy is particularly apparent in relation to cooperation on energy policy. The island of Ireland has had a single electricity market since 2007 so there exists a high degree of interdependence between the Republic of Ireland and Northern Ireland. This system has brought "considerable benefits to Northern Ireland, joining two small and relatively inefficient systems, to create greater economies of scale, cheaper electricity prices and improved security of supply" (House of Commons 2017: 17). The new *integrated* single electricity market on the island of Ireland is due to come into operation in 2018. Brexit, however, has prompted serious questions about the viability of this next phase of energy market integration. If the UK is to be outside the EU's internal energy market, this may lead to higher energy prices and reduced security of supply. There are also potential costs to Northern Ireland related to its dependence on fuel imports to generate electricity. Tariffs on imported gas, coal or oil are likely to impact negatively on Northern Ireland's competitiveness. And there is a degree of uncertainty in relation to future

EU funding support for the North–South interconnector and energy storage facilities.

Brexit, Northern Ireland and EU funding

The future of other EU funding supports to Northern Ireland is similarly unclear. The performance of Northern Ireland's regional economy has been underpinned by EU support. In their joint letter to the prime minister in August 2016, the first minister and deputy first minister note that Northern Ireland has received approximately €13 billion in total EU funding since 1994. For the funding period 2014–20, Northern Ireland receives the second largest amount of EU funding in terms of percentage of regional GDP. During the 2000–2006 funding period, however, Northern Ireland receipts from the structural funds outstripped those of any other part of the UK (see Figure 3.1).

EU financial support for Northern Ireland comes in a number of different forms. Structural funding has been used to support economic development, including measures to develop key infrastructure projects and initiatives to encourage private sector activity. Peace funding has aimed to support the consolidation of peace in Northern Ireland and the achievement of reconciliation. Other funding support includes the cross-border Interreg programme, rural development initiatives and direct payments to farmers (see Table 3.3). In total, Northern Ireland has been allocated €3,533 million in EU support for the funding period 2014–20. This is slightly more than for the 2007–13 funding period, when Northern Ireland received €3,449 million in EU financial support (see House of Lords 2016: 45).

Northern Ireland has also been awarded competitive funding for research through the FP7 and its successor Horizon 2020, the Competitiveness and Innovation programme, the Life+ programme, the Culture programme and the Trans-European Transport Network.[3]

---

3. During the period 2010–12, the draw down of FP7 funding was over £16 million. The figures for other competitive programmes however, including the Competitiveness and Innovation programme, and the Life+ and Culture programmes, were substantially less (see Northern Ireland Assembly Research and Information Service 2013). From 2007, the Northern Ireland–EU Taskforce (NITF) actively encouraged the Northern Ireland administration to work to increase Northern Ireland's drawdown of resources from competitive EU funds.

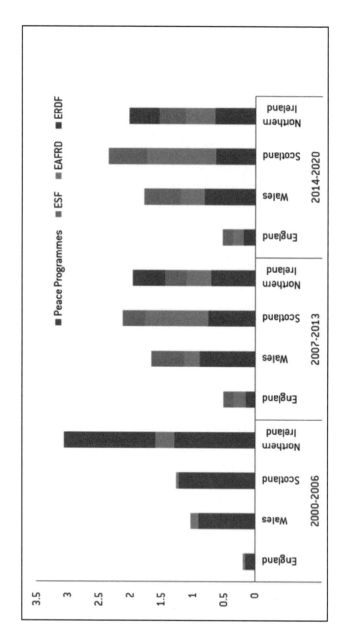

Figure 3.1 EU funds broken down by UK region, percentage of regional GDP

Source: Huttl and Romero (2016).

Table 3.3 EU co-funded programmes in Northern Ireland 2014–20

Programme	EU Allocation (€m)
Peace IV Programme: European Territorial Cooperation Programme Ireland–United Kingdom (Northern Ireland-Border Region of Ireland)	€229.1
ERDF: Investment for Growth and Jobs Programme for Northern Ireland	€308.0
Interreg VA: European Territorial Cooperation Programme United Kingdom–Ireland (Ireland-Northern Ireland-Western Scotland)	€240.3
ESF: Northern Ireland European Social Fund Programme	€205.2
CAP: Direct Payments (Pillar 1)	€2,299.0
CAP: Rural Development Programme (Pillar 2)	€228.0
European Maritime and Fisheries Fund	€23.5
Total	€3,533.1

Source: House of Lords (2016: 45–6).

The benefits of EU financial assistance to Northern Ireland have been considerable (Budd 2017: 122): "The loss of annual EU support funding of about £500 million per annum (about one-third of total GVA) would have a significant impact on the contribution of this sector to the Northern Ireland economy".

Importantly, the advantages of EU financial support have been more than just economic in scope: "Successive programmes may have explicitly aimed to improve economic performance, but they also sought to achieve political and social benefits" (Murphy 2014: 50). Given that the Northern Ireland economy is more dependent on EU funding than any other part of the UK, the loss of support that Brexit entails could have a devastating impact (House of Lords 2016: 44). Crucially, this impact will be both economic and political, threatening the continuation of large infrastructural investment, cross-border cooperation and mechanisms for supporting peace and reconciliation. Brexit also challenges the survival of a number of organizations across the voluntary and community sector in particular, which are dependent on EU financial support. There are no guarantees that the UK government would replicate or approximate EU funding support to Northern Ireland long-term.[4] A generous and novel financial support system that underpins post-conflict stability may be lost at a time when the need to address Northern Ireland's "negative peace" is at its most intense.

Studies of the economic impact of Brexit on Northern Ireland tend to be predominantly negative in tone and analysis. Those who support Brexit, however, are more buoyant about the potential opportunities available after the UK leaves the EU. The DUP has argued that although Northern Ireland has strong trading relations with the EU and Republic of Ireland, the most important market for Northern Ireland is in fact the UK. Moreover, the likelihood is that Northern Ireland will continue to trade with its European neighbours after Brexit, although the terms of that trading relationship remain unclear. There are also opportunities for Northern Ireland to seize future prospects to expand trade with other parts of the world. In an evidence session to the House of Commons Northern Ireland Affairs Committee, former Special Advisor to the First Minister of Northern Ireland 1998–2002, Dr Graham Gudgin noted: "Northern Ireland manufacturing already sells twice as much to the rest of the world outside the EU as it does to the continental EU. Those rest-of-the-world markets, many of which are in Asia, are faster growing than the EU" (3 February 2016). In the same evidence session, Gudgin suggested that the Peace programme and structural funds are not that important. On the whole however, this type of positive analysis does not enjoy substantial traction in Northern Ireland.

A key problem in determining the impact of Brexit is the lack of clarity and certainty about the terms of any future trade deal between the UK and the EU. This limits the extent to which the definitive consequences of Brexit can be identified. Nevertheless, the bulk of studies suggest that regardless of what deal is struck, that is hard Brexit or soft Brexit, Northern Ireland faces pronounced risks and profound challenges. These will probably be all the more severe if the UK leaves the EU with no deal.

---

4. In a communication to the European Council in early December 2017, the European Commission (2017: 9) indicated that the Peace and Interreg programmes should continue in Northern Ireland beyond the current programming period.

The economics of Brexit and the politics of Northern Ireland

The economic impact of Brexit cannot be disentangled from Northern Ireland's political situation. There is a link between EU membership and economic and political stability in Northern Ireland, and Brexit exposed its scope and effect. Upsetting this link presented economic and political risks that challenge a delicate peace settlement and unsettle fragile community relations.

Brexit and the Irish border

For Northern Ireland, the border between it and the Republic of Ireland matters deeply and has varied meanings, both concrete and symbolic. Its economic meaning is clear. The effective removal of border controls from the late 1980s facilitated the free movement of trade and people, a development that brought tangible economic benefits in terms of reduced transaction costs and increased trade (some of it based on complex supply chains). But the border has additional symbolic resonance that goes beyond dry economic calculation. The very existence of the border is at the heart of Northern Ireland's constitutional argument. In a political context, its key significance is its effect on identity, politics and the constitution (see Gormley-Heenan & Aughey 2017). Since the 1990s, a series of important developments have helped to depoliticize the border: these include the peace process, the resultant stabilization of political and communal relations, the demilitarization of the border region, and in particular, the signing of the 1998 Belfast Agreement, which created cross-border institutions designed to respond to identity issues. The consequence of removing the physical demarcation of the border was immensely important for the expression of nationalist identity in Northern Ireland.

All of these developments were implemented against the backdrop of UK and Irish membership of the EU. In an evidence session to the House of Commons Northern Ireland Affairs Committee, Irish Ambassador to the UK, Dan Mulhall, noted that common membership of the EU was a crucial framework within which the transformation of border politics took place (4 February 2016). The EU context was politically important for the peace process, but it was also economically significant for the way in which the SEM and the commitment of structural funding supported growth in Northern Ireland. The creation of the single market, in particular, facilitated the opening up of the trade border between North and South and the eradication of barriers at the border. The physical manifestation of the border effectively disappeared and impediments to movement on the island were removed. The emergent all-island dimension to economic development facilitated by the creation of cross-border institutions has been mutually beneficial for both parts of the island. The EU became an agency of economic change, and part of a process that complimented and buttressed other domestic political developments. Brexit, however, upends this state of affairs by challenging these arrangements and possibly resulting in the reimposition of some sort of (economic) border regime. A physical border between Northern Ireland and the Republic of Ireland signals a visible (if not literal) return to the so-called "borders of the past". It is a stark reminder of the Troubles when the two parts of the island were divided by a physical border infrastructure. Any new boundaries resulting from Brexit signals that the two parts of the island are now facing divergent futures: the Republic of Ireland within the EU, and Northern Ireland outside it. The political impact is potentially profound because it would impose a literal and a metaphorical distance between the two parts of the island. Nationalists have the most to lose in this context. SDLP leader Colum Eastwood notes (House of Lords 2016: 43):

> This is a huge constitutional change that is happening without our consent. For us, the Good Friday Agreement was about breaking down borders, further integrating across the island and working democratically in the absence of violence or intimidation towards our political aspirations. To take that away – to take the common EU membership we had with the south of Ireland away – has a tremendous destabilising effect on the Northern nationalist psyche … this shakes northern Nationalism to the core.

Nationalist identity was accommodated by EU membership, which allowed for the expression of a common Irish identity within a broader shared European context. In dissolving borders between north and south, the EU also facilitated the operation of cross-border

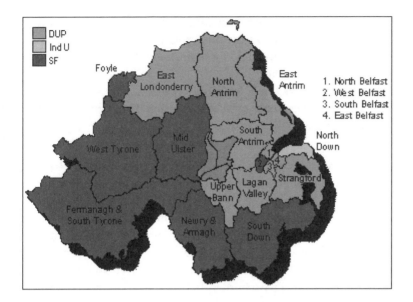

Figure 3.2 The 2017 Westminster election result in Northern Ireland

Source: "The 2017 Westminster elections in Northern Ireland", available at: http://www.ark.ac.uk/elections/fw17.html (accessed 2 February 2018).

institutions. Agreement on the creation of these institutions was a particularly important dimension of the Belfast Agreement for nation-alists because it gave practical expression to their nationalist identity and political preferences. EU financial support for the border region has also been instrumental in helping to revitalize underdeveloped borderland areas and in promoting cross-community and cross-border cooperation. Brexit puts critical achievements of the Northern Ireland peace process to the test and halts access to EU supporting mechanisms. And importantly, it does so without the popular support of the people of Northern Ireland, a majority of whom voted Remain. This new reality poses questions about the meaning and effect of the Belfast Agreement for nationalists because Brexit alters its capacity to meet and satisfy their legitimate political aspirations.

A study by Hayward (2017a: 13) for the Irish Central Border Area Network (ICBAN) notes that just one year after the EU referendum, Brexit is having an impact on the border area:

> Brexit is already having an effect in respondents' comfort in living on one side of the border and working on the other, in their confidence in doing business on the other side of the border, and in their view of the UK as a welcoming place for residence/work/study for Irish citizens … Frontier workers and some businesses are already feeling the effects of Brexit, particularly in the exchange rate.

In this context, the economic effects of Brexit are felt by both unionists and nationalists, and equally the impact is felt on both sides of the border. However, there is a greater concentration of nationalists in the border region. Figure 3.2 demonstrates that nationalist electoral support is at its strongest in border constituencies (and also in Mid Ulster and West Belfast). And it is nationalists who tend to feel more politically and psychologically aggrieved about the possible reimposition of a hard border. In the context of Brexit, Northern Ireland's economic position and political condition are inextricably intertwined.

Brexit and inequality in Northern Ireland

The severity of the impact of Brexit for the Northern Ireland economy will depend on what type of trade relationship the UK will have with the EU after it leaves the Union. However, regardless of what type of Brexit deal is reached, the various analyses suggest that leaving the EU will entail pronounced economic consequences for Northern Ireland. The gravity of the Brexit effect is also linked to the wider economic context. Northern Ireland's economy suffers from some specific difficulties, including persistent structural problems and the legacy of the conflict. The achievement of the peace process and the signing of a peace settlement in the 1990s were not just politically and constitutionally significant, they were also interpreted as important moments in Northern Ireland's economic rejuvenation. Political leaders linked peace in Northern Ireland to increased opportunities for economic advancement. The hope was that the absence of conflict would remove structural barriers to economic growth that would in turn further reinforce political progress. The so-called "peace dividend" was predicated on Northern

Ireland's increased ability to attract inward investment and to create jobs (O'hearn 2008: 102). The promise of economic revival, however, rang hollow. Despite some increase in FDI, the influx of investment was not extensive, and crucially nor was it evenly distributed. Coulter (2014) identifies a post-conflict Northern Ireland economy that was character-ized by an inflated public sector, lower than average wages in the pri-vate sector, a high worklessness rate, a heavy reliance on welfare and an increasing wealth differential. By methodically identifying and detailing the performance of the manufacturing and services sectors in Northern Ireland ten years after the ceasefires, O'hearn (2008) demonstrates the extent to which the peace dividend has been largely illusory. To the extent that it is discernible, the peace dividend has accrued to the wealthier sec-tions of Northern Ireland society. Those most affected by the conflict have not been beneficiaries of economic growth. Unemployment levels in Northern Ireland's most disadvantaged wards remain persistently high: "the areas now worst affected by poverty were those worst hit by violence during the period of the Troubles" (Campbell *et al.* 2016: 7; see also O'hearn 2008: 107). Even though "horizontal inequalities" between Catholics and Protestants have been addressed, marginalized commu-nities, from both the Catholic/nationalist and the Protestant/loyalist tradition, remain socio-economically marginalized long after the violence has halted. Their situation worsened further with the onset of the global financial crisis from 2008. Northern Ireland's construction industry – one of the few sectors to experience growth after 1994 – was plunged into recession, and the imposition of austerity in the form of public spend-ing and welfare cuts exacerbated the position of the most marginalized. Inequality across the UK worsened during this period. Between 2008 and 2013, the UK's poorest regions were subject to the worst effects of the crisis and Northern Ireland fell squarely into this category. The region's private sector shrank by almost 1.5 per cent on an annual basis during this period (Springford 2015: 2). Figure 3.3. illustrates the reduction in private sector output between 2008 and 2013. Output has rallied since then, with the weakness of sterling pushing up export orders and increas-ing private sector activity.

On the whole, however, Northern Ireland continues to be one of the most disadvantaged parts of the UK (see Figure 3.4). A study by Knox confirms that across a range of indicators including education, health, welfare, crime and social welfare/worklessness, the result is

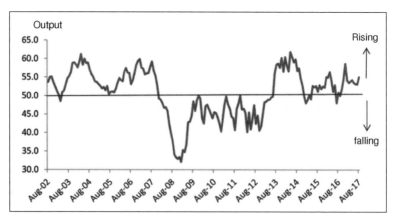

Figure 3.3 Northern Ireland business activity index 2002–17
Source: Ramsey (2017).

an increasingly unequal society: "In short, there has been no peace dividend for those living in the most deprived areas of Northern Ireland, in fact their quality of life appears to be marginally declining" (Knox 2016: 487).

Brexit's economic impact will be felt in terms of reduced GDP, a fall-off in FDI, a decrease in trade and a loss of EU funding support. Springford (2015: 6) notes: "the poorest regions of the UK [will] feel the pain". Even at the regional level, however, the effects of Brexit will trickle down and be experienced differently by sectors, by sub-regions, by class, by demographic profile and by community. Herein lies a further danger for Northern Ireland. Underdeveloped and socio-economically deprived communities will be more adversely affected by Brexit than affluent communities. In Northern Ireland, this suggests that those areas that suffered disproportionate socio-economic hardship during (and after) the Troubles face additional Brexit related economic challenges. The effect of this is to further economically marginalize those communities that have been most susceptible to conflict and violence. Local people in these predominantly working-class areas report feeling a sense of frustration, hopelessness, disillusionment and being "left behind" (Holland & Rabrenovic 2017: 234). The fact that such sentiments are expressed and felt by *both* Catholic/nationalist and Protestant/loyalist communities has not facilitated the emergence of a cross-community working-class movement or political party.

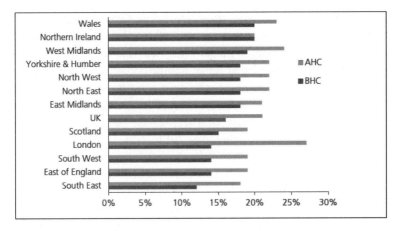

Figure 3.4 Percentage of population (all ages) in relative low income
2013/14–2015/16

Note: Income can be measured before housing costs (BHC) are deducted or after housing costs (AHC) are deducted.

Source: McGuinness (2016).

This means that discontent is therefore channelled through existing political and ethno-sectarian frames. The constitutional issue becomes entangled with socio-economic distress and feeds a mentality that perpetuates polarization of the two communities. At its most intense, dissatisfaction and discontent may spill over and prompt deeper visceral responses to hardship, including aggression and violence. In this context, the impact of a Brexit-related economic downturn is potentially dire not just for the fragile Northern Ireland economy but for the fragile Northern Ireland peace process too. The interplay between the economic effects of the UK withdrawal from the EU, and stability within and between communities in Northern Ireland is significant. The links between Brexit and economic stability play out in particularly sensitive and highly politicized ways in Northern Ireland.

Brexit and the Northern Ireland peace process

If we consider the way in which the economic impact of Brexit has both political and socio-economic consequences, it is clear that it creates an undesirable environment in a region that is emerging from conflict.

Brexit unsettles a hard-won constitutional settlement and simultaneously, for certain vulnerable sections of Northern Ireland society, provokes economic instability, undermines welfare and reinforces a sense of disaffection. The charge that Brexit has the potential to endanger the peace process was roundly rejected by those campaigners who favoured a UK exit from the EU. However, the effect of the multitude of forces that Brexit unleashed in Northern Ireland has the potential to be both divisive and dangerous (Holland & Rabrenovic 2017: 240):

> The consequent growth in class inequalities within post-colonial societies with histories of ethno-political or ethno-religious conflict thus holds the potential to fuel simmering mentalities of threat and loss which risk taking sectarian, racist or otherwise dangerous forms – especially when promoted by ethno-political entrepreneurs.

Insofar as economic grievances are perceived to cut across ethno-national identities and aspirations, the impact of Brexit may have a sectarian dimension and an acutely political effect. Economic disaffection and marginalization may fuel a push for political and constitutional change. For example, in this context, nationalist/republican communities may be persuaded that their economic (and political and social and cultural) well-being is better catered for by the achievement of a united Ireland. This formed part of Sinn Féin's immediate response to the EU referendum result, although it has enjoyed limited traction since then. Nevertheless, increasingly disaffected and economically disadvantaged nationalists/republicans may be more responsive to this type of rhetoric in the future. There is also the fear that communities may be open to manipulation by paramilitary forces. The severity of the economic impact of Brexit will be a decisive factor in determining the extent to which (dissident) paramilitaries may be able to exercise influence over local communities. Similar forces are evident for unionists/loyalists. The political identity of unionism tends towards being "against" nationalists and so it does not have a secure ideological, political or cultural basis. Numerically the size of the unionist community is also in decline. These factors feed into unionist ethno-political insecurities and create a community that is perpetually defensive and distrustful. In the context of Brexit, those insecurities are bolstered by nationalist support for Remain (which clashes with unionist support for Leave) and by the marginalization effects of the UK withdrawal from the EU. Such developments breed resentment and may see unionists/loyalists adopt hardened political positions that hark back to the dark days of the Troubles. In all this, the potential for communal polarization is heightened, creating an environment that is ripe for paramilitary exploitation.

A tenuous situation is complicated by the suspension of devolved institutions in Northern Ireland. The breakdown of political relations between Sinn Féin and the DUP was born out of a deep omnipresent sense of mutual distrust. The political vacuum further fuels the seeds of distrust and allows lingering divisions to foment. The fundamentals of a "negative peace" remain intact, and are perhaps even being reinforced. The apparent dysfunction of the Stormont Assembly[5] and the weak Northern Ireland engagement with the UK centre meant limits to how much the UK was fully aware of Northern Ireland interests. This potentially toughens the resolve of disaffected nationalists to seek alternative constitutional remedies for Northern Ireland's future, prompting unionist opposition and possibly communal tensions and political instability.

Warnings about the impact of Brexit on the peace process were generally underplayed during the EU referendum campaign. Since the vote, however, the need to ensure continued peace in Northern Ireland has been a focal point of the Irish government's approach to the Brexit negotiations. "Protecting the Northern Ireland peace process" is one of the Irish government's four Brexit priorities (Irish Government 2017: 19):

> The preservation of the gains of peace over the past 20 years must be a priority for the EU in the upcoming negotiations with the UK and we must ensure that there is no disruption to the integrity of the peace settlement achieved through the Good Friday Agreement.

---

5. Following the failure of Northern Ireland's political parties to reach agreement on reinstituting the suspended devolved institutions, then Secretary of State James Brokenshire moved the *Northern Ireland Budget Bill* in November 2017. The budget is normally the responsibility of the devolved institutions, but given the continued suspension, the Westminster bill was required to maintain public services in Northern Ireland that were otherwise threatened by resources running out.

The UK government's *Position Paper on Northern Ireland and Ireland* (HM Government 2017a) contains a similar commitment to the peace process and the Belfast Agreement. The Irish government, however, has arguably been more vocal in highlighting the potential for Brexit to lead to renewed conflict in Northern Ireland. In a speech to the European People's Party (EPP), the then Irish Taoiseach Enda Kenny linked the introduction of a hard border to the potential for violence. He noted that in the past a hard border on the island of Ireland (*Newstalk*, 11 May 2017):

> brought with it sectarianism and thirty years of real difficulties where 3,000 people lost their lives. [With] acts of terrorism, indiscriminate bombings and all of that trouble and tragedy that it brought on so many families. We do not want a return to that sectarian issue – and therefore politically we cannot have a border as applied before.

During his first visit to Northern Ireland as Taoiseach in August 2017, Leo Varadkar, delivered a speech at Queen's University Belfast in which he also equated the former border between north and south as having been "a barrier to trade, prosperity and peace". Nationalists in Northern Ireland similarly depicted Brexit in this manner. Former British prime ministers and Irish Taoisigh also warned that Brexit threatens the Northern Ireland peace process.[6] In contrast, unionists strongly dispute any link between Brexit, economic decline and the renewal of hostilities in Northern Ireland. During the EU referendum campaign, DUP leader Arlene Foster "condemned the narrative that portrayed Brexit as a threat to the peace process in Northern Ireland" (McCann & Hainsworth 2017: 330). This underlines the very fundamental differences between the two communities in Northern Ireland about how to interpret Brexit. The UK decision to leave the EU opened up new differences and divisions in Northern Ireland that entail implications for Northern Ireland's future. Polarizing views about Brexit's intertwined economic and political effects challenge Northern Ireland's delicate communal relations.

---

6. This includes former British Prime Ministers Tony Blair and John Major, and former Irish Taoisigh Bertie Ahern and John Bruton.

Conclusion

The House of Lords European Union Committee noted in its report *Brexit: UK–Irish Relations* that "the risks to the Northern Ireland economy posed by Brexit probably outweigh the opportunities" (2016: 17). This analysis is widely reflected in other studies. The peculiarities of the Northern Ireland economy and its low performance levels laid the foundations for Brexit to be particularly harshly felt. The effects are felt at the macroeconomic level with a reduction in the GDP rate and downward growth rates. Trade, inward investment and the agri-food sector are likely to be among the biggest casualties, although the precise terms of the future UK–EU trading relationship will have a bearing on the extent of the implications. Northern Ireland is also set to lose structural funding and CAP support.

The economic impact of Brexit cannot be divorced from the political dynamics it is unleashing. The Northern Ireland economy's structural problems limit the extent to which the region can meet the broader challenges associated with leaving the EU. Future weak economic performance undermines attempts to fix the peculiarities of the local economy, and limits the extent to which persistent structural difficulties can be met. Those who voted for Brexit were those who felt "left behind", and it is this more vulnerable section of society that stands to gain little, in economic terms, from the UK exit from the EU. It is this cohort of citizens in Northern Ireland that also endured the worst long-term effects of the Troubles and experienced inequality. The so-called "peace dividend" was largely illusory and the EU referendum vote has brought no Brexit dividend either. Those who stand to lose most from Brexit are those who are most economically disadvantaged. There is political disaffection too. The reimposition of the border linked to UK removal from the SEM shatters one of the central tenets of Ireland's political landscape post Belfast Agreement. The blurring (near eradication) of the physical border has been particularly important for the development of the all-island economy, and perhaps more especially for nationalist identity. Taken together, these developments threaten to undermine the peace process by providing a space and a narrative that may be seized upon by those who link their discontentment to Brexit and who observe political and constitutional change as a route to meeting the challenges they face. More sinisterly, paramilitaries are ripe to exploit this kind of precarious situation.

A deep analysis of Northern Ireland and Brexit suggests that the possibility of economic decline that Brexit entails threatens not only Northern Ireland's economic future, but also its political, social and constitutional stability. Brexit produces a clash between Northern Ireland's introverted politics and its political economy, which imperils the limited economic gains and the substantial political gains of the peace process. In Northern Ireland, Brexit demonstrates the complex (sometimes toxic) interplay between economics and politics. Various understandings and interpretations of these dynamics were displayed by Northern Ireland political parties, the devolved institutions, the two governments, civil society and the EU, both before and after the EU referendum. Chapter 4 asks "who speaks for Northern Ireland?" and queries what they say, how they communicate and ultimately, what impact they have had on determining Northern Ireland's future outside the EU.

4

Who speaks for Northern Ireland?

The EU referendum result was met with widespread shock and surprise. The narrow win for Leave was largely unexpected. The following day the *Belfast Telegraph* (25 June 2016) front page declared "A step into the unknown". The value of sterling had plummeted in response to the vote and the UK Prime Minister David Cameron had resigned. In Northern Ireland, the immediate response from unionism and nationalism exposed a clear difference between the two communities. DUP First Minister Arlene Foster declared: "I think this is a good result for the United Kingdom. Our nation state has made a clear definition as to where they want to go forward." Deputy First Minister, Sinn Féin's Martin McGuinness, reacted very differently and viewed the result as justification for pushing a different future for Northern Ireland: "I think there is a democratic imperative for a border poll". The strong vote in favour of Remain in Scotland was interpreted by First Minister Nicola Sturgeon as: "a sign of divergence between Scotland and large parts of the rest of the UK in how we see our place in the world". For its part, the Irish government was dismayed by the result and the then Taoiseach Enda Kenny moved to immediately recall the Irish parliament. In a joint statement by EU leaders[1] and the Netherlands presidency of the EU, the three presidents and prime minister expressed regret at the decision but were clear in their commitment to the future of the European project. They voiced a desire to see the UK move swiftly to give effect to the referendum result. A combination of regret and resilience also featured in the responses of German Chancellor Angela Merkel and her French counterpart, François Hollande, to the vote.

---

1. The EU leaders referred to here are: European Commission President, Jean Claude Juncker; European Parliament President, Martin Schulz; and European Council President, Donald Tusk.

The referendum result meant that the UK was now facing a period of political and economic turmoil and possibly sustained instability. The mammoth and unprecedented task of steering the UK out of the EU was to be led by the new Prime Minister Theresa May, who was installed in July 2016. Having campaigned for the UK to remain in the EU, her starting position was to declare "Brexit means Brexit", an ambiguous message but one that hinted at a possible hard Brexit. For Northern Ireland, this meant that the early signs were ominous. A hard Brexit threatened access to the single market and free movement on the island of Ireland, and it also risked antagonizing a fragile political accommodation.

The narrowness of the Leave victory and the deep discords that it revealed exposed the divided nature of the UK. The division manifested itself in many ways: "society ... had, on the issues of EU membership and immigration, become divided by social class, generation and geography" (Goodwin & Heath 2016: 324). In geographic terms, the Leave vote was heavily concentrated in England. In contrast, all 32 of Scotland's local authorities chose Remain, as did most of London and a majority of Northern Ireland's 18 constituencies. The Remain vote was also more heavily supported by younger voters while those in the older age brackets were more likely to vote Leave. In a similar vein, those who were pro-Brexit were generally in the lower socio-economic categories and less educated. Better educated and more affluent voters tended to support Remain.[2]

The marked fault lines that the referendum result revealed are part of the complexity of the Brexit challenge. The magnitude of the exit process was not helped by the severe lack of preparedness for a Leave outcome. From a Northern Ireland perspective, the absence of preparations was one thing, but the failure to acknowledge and appreciate the precise nature of the grave challenges that Brexit meant for the region was quite another. The UK neglect of the extent to which Brexit threatens serious economic and political consequences for Northern Ireland has been a troubling hallmark of the UK's Brexit approach and strategy. This chapter details if and how Northern Ireland issues have

---

2. A series of linear regression models conducted by Goodwin and Heath (2016) after the vote found that lower educational levels and higher age profile had a significant effect on the level of support for leaving the EU.

been addressed by the various parties to the Brexit process, including the UK government, the Northern Ireland administration, the Irish government and the EU. It determines which issues have been prioritized and which have been overlooked, and assesses the consequences of this for Northern Ireland's political and economic stability.

Representing all of the UK? The British government's approach to Brexit

No member state has ever previously triggered Article 50, the legal provision that facilitates the process of departure from the EU.[3] There is, therefore, no template for how to approach the gargantuan challenge of extracting a member state from the multiplicity of legal, economic and political commitments that EU membership entails. The sheer enormity and scale of the task only became clear in the months following the referendum as the precise detail of the Brexit process began to crystallize. It is clear that the UK faces an extraordinary and unprecedented task in honouring the referendum result. The conditions within which the UK government is working towards Brexit are less than ideal. The UK electorate is divided and polarized and so is national politics. Schisms are evident not just between parties, but within parties too. Both the Conservative Party and the Labour Party lack cohesion. The problem is particularly acute for the Tories among whom a core group of Brexiteers have made the prime minister's grip on power tenuous, especially after the punishing general election result in 2017 that saw the party's slim majority dwindle further. There has also been disruption within the UK's "permanent government", namely the civil service. The restructuring of government departments, a reshuffling of staff, and a small number of resignations by leading civil servants[4]

---

3. Article 50 of the Lisbon Treaty (which came into force in 2009) establishes the right of a member state to withdraw from the EU.
4. For example, one of the UK's top leading civil servants and British ambassador to the EU, Sir Ivan Rogers, stepped down from his role in Brussels in early 2017. In his resignation email to UKRep staff Sir Rogers noted:
   Serious multilateral negotiating experience is in short supply in Whitehall, and that is not the case in the Commission or in the Council. The government

have unsettled and disturbed the administrative landscape at a time of intense contestation. This meant that the UK faced the challenge of Brexit at a time of political volatility and administrative change. This hampered the government's room for manoeuvre and its ability to confront certain issues. Arguably however, the lack of preparedness pre-dated the referendum. A report by the House of Commons Foreign Affairs Committee slammed the British government's lack of contingency planning in advance of the vote (2016: 3): "The previous Government's considered view not to instruct key Departments including the FCO [Foreign and Commonwealth Office] to plan for the possibility that the electorate would vote to leave the EU amounted to gross negligence". The prime minister's office under Cameron had resisted instructing key government departments to produce contingency plans for fear of leaks, which may then have undermined the Remain campaign. An overall lack of preparation, however, may have been even more acute in the case of Northern Ireland.

In the broader UK context, Northern Ireland has always been "a place apart".[5] Geographically distinct from the rest of the UK, the region's experience of conflict and communal divide, and its fixation on the constitutional question lent an air of particularity to the place. The 1994 ceasefires, the signing of the Belfast Agreement four years later, and the recent perception of peace has seen the British government take a step back from what was once a deep engagement with Northern Ireland politics. For almost a decade, this detachment has characterized the British government's approach to Northern Ireland (see Chapter 2). In the lead-in to the EU referendum, this disengagement reduced the ability of the British government to know, understand and appreciate what Brexit meant for Northern Ireland. This was apparent when a delegation of unionists met with then Prime Minister David Cameron

---

will only achieve the best for the country if it harnesses the best experience we have – a large proportion of which is concentrated in UKRep – and negotiates resolutely. Senior ministers, who will decide on our positions, issue by issue, also need from you detailed, unvarnished – even where this is uncomfortable – and nuanced understanding of the views, interests and incentives of the other 27. (*The Guardian*, 4 January 2017)

5. *A Place Apart* is the title of a book by author Dervla Murphy. It was published in 1978 and recounts Murphy's travels and encounters in Northern Ireland during the 1970s.

to discuss contingency plans for the Irish border in the event of a Leave vote. UUP MEP Jim Nicholson who attended the meeting was taken aback by the prime minister's ambivalence (Rothwell 2017):

> I asked him [David Cameron] what would happen to the bor-
> der … and he said to me, what do you mean? He thought it
> was for the Leave side to answer that question … There was
> never any thinking on the government's part on the problems
> that would occur. They thought they were going to win [the
> EU referendum].

Former Irish foreign minister and leader of Fianna Fáil, Micheál Martin, was also struck by what he saw as the British government's "naïve" approach to the referendum. An assumption of victory had allowed a blasé approach to the campaign to develop and this prevented any serious engagement with key issues (see Connolly 2017a: 12–13). Those who supported Brexit during the referendum campaign had little to say about Northern Ireland and the border issue either. Former Irish Foreign Affairs Minister, Charlie Flanagan, alluded to this when he spoke in Belfast in late 2015:

> I just suspect that the situation of this particular border hasn't
> figured that highly in the thinking of many of those who so
> strongly favour a British withdrawal from the EU. This was
> probably not a prime consideration of theirs. And it's prob-
> ably low down the list in the minds of those who dream about
> a post-Brexit Britain.

The 2016 UKIP Northern Ireland Assembly election manifesto makes little detailed reference to how the land border between Northern Ireland and the Republic of Ireland would be affected following a vote to leave. Similarly, on a visit to Northern Ireland during the EU referendum campaign, then UKIP leader, Nigel Farage, claimed that Brexit posed no threat to Northern Ireland, and that soft border arrangements would probably be maintained in the event of a Leave vote (*Irish Times*, 2 March 2016). The pro-Brexit DUP was also sanguine in its analysis. Warnings about the possible imposition of border controls and checkpoints were dismissed as "scaremongering" by DUP MP Sammy

Wilson who claimed Remain campaigners were "telling outright lies, [employing] scare tactics, treating the public with disdain" (*Belfast Telegraph*, 1 June 2016). A hard border was viewed as incompatible with the interests of both Northern Ireland and the Republic of Ireland, and therefore in the event of a vote to leave the EU, the DUP believed that its imposition was unlikely.

A lack of clarity and consensus around the specific Northern Ireland-Brexit issues before the referendum persisted after the referendum. There is admittedly acknowledgement of Northern Ireland (and the Republic of Ireland) in a number of UK documents, but in all these, there is little precise detail about how to navigate the complexity of the Irish border. Prime Minister May's letter to European Council President Donald Tusk in March 2017 triggering Article 50 made specific reference to Ireland and to protecting the peace process in Northern Ireland. This echoes one of the 12 principles contained in the UK Government's White Paper (see HM Government 2017b). The UK government's *Position Paper on Northern Ireland and Ireland* (HM Government 2017a), published in August 2017, outlines a commitment to safeguard the Belfast Agreement and stability in Northern Ireland. The document, however, like earlier UK government pronouncements, does not include any significant amount of detail in relation to how to prevent a hard border. In theory, a hard Brexit necessitates a hard border between the Republic of Ireland and Northern Ireland. In practice, pro-and anti-Brexiteers in Northern Ireland, as well as the UK and Irish governments, are keen to see the management of the Irish border remain as close as possible to current arrangements. In this context, and given the specific circumstances that pertain on the island of Ireland, the EU is willing to be flexible in relation to how a new form of border management might be developed and implemented. The key stumbling block is the lack of clarity and consensus in relation to the design and implementation of such a flexible arrangement.

The feasibility of some of the proposals put forward has been rejected by the UK, which has consistently been opposed to calls for special treatment for Northern Ireland – effectively a type of bespoke arrangement that would recognize Northern Ireland's specific circumstances and the unique issues they give rise to. However, treating Northern Ireland as "special" is anathema to unionists who do not wish Northern

Ireland to be treated differently to other parts of the UK. They are supported in this regard by the British government. The former Secretary of State for Northern Ireland, James Brokenshire, has repeatedly stated that this would be the wrong approach. The British government's opposition to any form of "special status" for Northern Ireland is strongly supported by the unionist community, but rejected by nationalists. The result was something of a stalemate. In his press statement following the fifth round of Article 50 negotiations with the UK (October 2017), Michel Barnier noted some advances in relation to the CTA and mapping cross-border cooperation, but made no mention of progress on the border issue. Following the sixth round of Brexit negotiations, Barnier noted "the unique situation on the island of Ireland requires specific solutions" (10 November 2017). This statement followed the leaking of a paper the previous day that had been "carefully choreographed between the Irish Government and the EU Brexit Task Force" (Connolly 2017b). The controversial document suggested that the only way to avoid a hard border on the island of Ireland was for Northern Ireland to remain within the customs union and single market. The proposal was immediately denounced by the British government and the DUP. The document, however, was not a policy statement, but a working paper, albeit one designed to push the British government to address Irish issues before the final European Council summit of 2017. Phase one of the Brexit negotiations concluded in December 2017 with agreement between the EU negotiators and the UK government on the three components of the first negotiating phase: citizens' rights, the financial settlement and the dialogue on Ireland/Northern Ireland. The latter issue was intensely problematic. It highlighted the incompatibilities between the UK government's preference to leave the SEM and customs union, and a stated desire to avoid a hard border on the island of Ireland. The episode also exposed deep misunderstandings and/or poor communication between the Conservative Party negotiating team and the DUP. An agreed EU–UK paper was abandoned when the smaller party objected to the insinuation in the text that the deal facilitated moving the border to the Irish Sea. Agreement was eventually reached and detailed in an EU–UK joint report (8 December 2017). The report affirmed support for the peace process and Belfast Agreement, committed to avoiding the imposition of a hard border, and in the absence of agreed solutions, Article 50 of the Joint Report states:

the United Kingdom will ensure that no new regulatory barriers develop between Northern Ireland and the rest of the United Kingdom, unless, consistent with the 1998 Agreement, the Northern Ireland Executive and Assembly agree that distinct arrangements are appropriate for Northern Ireland. In all cases, the United Kingdom will continue to ensure the same unfettered access for Northern Ireland's businesses to the whole of the United Kingdom internal market.

The joint report provides some limited guarantees in relation to avoiding a hard border and respecting the Belfast Agreement, but it does not resolve the question of the Irish border.[6] The vagueness and haziness contained in the joint report kicked the border issue into phase two of the negotiations.

Northern Ireland and Brexit institutional initiatives

Following the introduction of devolution in 1999, the British government created intergovernmental structures to facilitate dialogue and discussion between the centre and the regions. A series of Joint Ministerial Committees (JMC) were focused around various sectoral themes. The JMC for Europe (JMC[E]) was one such structure, although it has been subject to accusations that it was not always mobilized to facilitate input from the devolved administrations. There have been frustrations about the limits to influence and the lack of discussion, accountability and follow-up that the current institutional and political set-up facilitates (see McEwen 2017). For example, there was no JMC[E] meeting in advance of the February 2016 European Council when then Prime Minister David Cameron agreed a settlement on EU reform. A new JMC[EN] was created in 2016. Its purpose was to allow the devolveds to contribute to the broader UK Brexit process. The utility of the new JMC, however, has been similarly criticized for the poor frequency and limited manner of engagement between central government and the devolveds on key issues and decisions (see House of Lords European

---

6. The joint report contains an important caveat: "nothing is agreed until everything is agreed".

Union Committee 2017). There has been particular dissatisfaction with the British government's failure to consult adequately with the regions on major Brexit developments, including the prime minister's decision to trigger Article 50 in March 2017 when she did not use the structure (or any other facility) to give the devolved administrations advance notice of her intention.

The JMC[EN] structure may have its flaws, but it does provide at least a partial means for the devolveds to communicate with central government. For Northern Ireland, however, even this opportunity was lost during the suspension of the institutions. Northern Ireland politicians did not attend meetings of the committee during this period and there were no Northern Ireland papers submitted.[7] Without political representation, Northern Ireland's voice was effectively absent. As the British government has shifted its attention away from Northern Ireland, its ability to know and appreciate the issues that are at stake is compromised. The lack of a functioning Northern Ireland Executive meant that there was no ready means of engaging with institutional channels designed to communicate information and positions. For Northern Ireland, the JMC[EN] was a lost political opportunity that was all the more disadvantageous given a gradual pattern of British detachment on the Northern Ireland issue.

Northern Ireland and Brexit negotiating opportunities

There are a range of ways in which the UK's devolved units influence the UK's Brexit process. The Scottish and Welsh executives both produced plans that set out their respective objectives and ambitions for the negotiating period (Scottish Government 2016 and Welsh Government 2017). Each government has identified, communicated and argued its case, not just at the national level, but also to the EU itself, and to other EU member states and regions. Unlike Scotland and Wales, Northern Ireland did not draft specific Brexit objectives and preferences for the region. Here again, the absence of a functioning Northern

---

7. The secretary of state for Northern Ireland (or parliamentary under-secretary) attended the JMC[EN] and a senior Northern Ireland civil servant also attended meetings during the period of suspension.

Ireland Executive hamstrung the emergence of a clear Northern Ireland position on Brexit. Even before the collapse of the Northern Ireland Executive in early 2017, the ability of the Northern Ireland administration to agree a position on Brexit was limited. A Northern Ireland Assembly motion on 17 October 2016 endorsing that there should be "legal recognition of the unique status of Northern Ireland and the circumstances on the island as part of the arrangements to leave the European Union" was defeated by a single vote. Forty-six MLAs voted in favour of the motion with 47 voting against. The vote reveals wholesale nationalist support for "unique status" and blanket unionist opposition. The fall of the Executive a few months further antagonized the situation. There was, in effect, a complete lack of political leadership on attending to Northern Ireland interests following the referendum vote and during the first Brexit negotiation phase. Of course, even had the Assembly and Executive been operational, the likelihood of an agreed Northern Ireland position emerging was not assured. However, even without a strong Northern Ireland position, the very fact of there being a functioning Executive and Assembly would at least have allowed Northern Ireland to be plugged into some of the wider opportunities for influencing and contributing to the Brexit process such as through the JMC[EN]. Northern Ireland also missed out on opportunities to collaborate on certain shared concerns. In July 2017, Scottish and Welsh leaders met with Chief EU Brexit Negotiator, Michel Barnier. With no Executive in place, Northern Ireland could not avail of this kind of access. Politicians from both sides of the political divide in Northern Ireland expressed concerns about their exclusion from such opportunities. DUP MP Jeffery Donaldson acknowledged that this situation is "most unfortunate to say the least" (*Belfast Telegraph*, 14 July 2017) while SDLP leader, Colum Eastwood, noted: "While Scotland and Wales meet with the EU lead, we are left without a voice at that table" (*Newsletter*, 13 July 2017).

There are other forums wherein discussion of the Brexit vote has been facilitated. Institutions created by the Belfast Agreement, the British–Irish Council (BIC) and the North/South Ministerial Council (NSMC) discussed the implications of Brexit for Ireland, the UK and its constituent parts. An Extraordinary Summit Meeting of the BIC was convened on 22 July 2016 to consider the outcome of the EU referendum. Participants reflected on how the result impacted on their regions. They also reaffirmed the importance of the Council in facilitating "harmonious and mutually beneficial relationships among the people of these islands" (BIC Communiqué, 22 July 2016). A further summit meeting in November 2016 developed these discussions and ministers went further in their view that the BIC assumed particular importance in the context of Brexit (BIC Communiqué, 25 November 2016): "Ministers agreed that the forthcoming developments underline the importance and value of the Council as a unique forum to share views, enhance cooperation and strengthen relationships".

The precise value of the BIC is unclear. Positive affirmations from BIC members is one thing, but the BIC does not meet regularly in summit format. At BIC summit meetings, the UK government is represented by territorial secretaries of state and parliamentary under-secretaries of state. The lower profile of British central government participants contrasts with the highest level of Irish government engagement in the form of the Taoiseach and minister for foreign affairs/minister for education/government chief whip. At the November 2017 BIC summit, there was no Northern Ireland representation owing to the suspension of the devolved institutions (although the UK government's representative was the secretary of state for Northern Ireland). According to a senior BIC official, the summit involves a flow of information from the UK central government to the other administrations. It is not necessarily a listening forum or one where an exchange of views and positions takes place. Coupled with the infrequency of its summit meetings and the low level of engagement by the British government, it is difficult to classify the BIC as an important or high-level forum wherein the British government can garner the views of the devolveds on key Brexit issues.

In line with the suspension of the Northern Ireland Assembly and Executive, the operation of the NSMC has also been suspended. Two plenary meetings of the NSMC took place during the period after the EU referendum and before suspension of the devolved institutions. The first meeting in July 2016 was somewhat overshadowed by evident tensions between the Northern Ireland First Minister Arlene Foster and Taoiseach Enda Kenny. In the days following the Brexit vote, members of the Irish government publically raised the idea of an all-island forum on Brexit that would involve all political parties, interest groups, citizens and stakeholders. However, the proposal had not been floated with the DUP before being publicized. At the NSMC meeting, DUP leader Arlene Foster rejected the proposal. She stated (see Connolly 2017a: 36): "I believe that there are more than enough mechanisms by which we can discuss these issues on a North–South basis. Frankly, I don't believe there are any mechanisms needed because we can lift the phone to each other on a daily basis if that were so needed."

Despite the DUP rejection of the Irish government's North–South civic dialogue proposal, the members of the NSMC did adopt a proactive approach to Brexit at both the plenary and sectoral levels. The Joint Communiqué following the July 2016 NSMC plenary meeting noted a number of priority areas where implications arise for both jurisdictions including:

- the economy and trade
- Northern Ireland and British Irish relations
- the Common Travel Area
- the EU.

Full sectoral audits of the impact of Brexit across government departments in the Republic of Ireland and Northern Ireland were undertaken, and bilateral cooperation between ministers, departments and officials was agreed. Ministers also agreed to increase the frequency of briefings on relevant EU matters provided by the Irish government and to intensify the close working relationship between the Irish Permanent Representation and the Northern Ireland Executive Office in Brussels. In terms of the border issue, the meeting did not include discussion of "special status" for Northern Ireland, and there was no conversation about Northern Ireland remaining in the EEA or EFTA (see Northern Ireland Assembly Official Report (Hansard), 22 November 2016). Participants avoided discussion of these more contentious and divisive issues concerning Northern Ireland's future post Brexit. The overarching discussion was pragmatic and focused on creating structures to enable officials to identify key issues and to gather relevant information. There was some expectation that "final priorities will be agreed by the next NSMC plenary for both pre-negotiation and negotiation phases". That NSMC, scheduled for Spring 2017, however, did not meet. It, and all other sectoral meetings, were halted when devolution was suspended in early 2017. Importantly however, this did not stop cooperation between civil servants, which continues apace. The lack of political leadership in Northern Ireland, however, remains problematic as it undermines the dynamism of the Council and the urgency of its work and deliberations. Its suspension also removes a potentially useful forum for cross-border discussion on Brexit. The Special EU Programmes [Implementation] Body (SEUPB), whose work is overseen by the NSMC, is a North–South body that stands to be profoundly affected by Brexit. The body is responsible for the implementation of the EU's PEACE IV and INTERREG V A structural fund programmes.[8] The possible loss of EU funding, however, threatens the future of this body and undermines a key area of cross-border cooperation. It remains unclear if the SEUPB will have responsibility for implementing future EU programmes (beyond 2020) and/or cross-border programmes funded jointly by the two governments and/or the EU.

Northern Ireland and the Brexit legislative process

On the day the UK leaves the EU, there is a need to ensure legal continuity in terms of the continued application of a substantial body of EU law. The Withdrawal Bill aims to achieve this continuity. The passage of the bill through parliament has been highly contentious and it has been subjected to a raft of amendments. Of the 300+ amendments, the bulk of these have been submitted by MPs from the devolved regions who fear the bill in its current form will centralize powers within the UK, and have a detrimental effect on the autonomy of the devolved assemblies. No amendment has been submitted by a Northern Ireland MP. The ten DUP MPs are shoring up the minority Conservative Party government and as part of the confidence-and-supply agreement have committed to support the Brexit process – the Withdrawal Bill is an important part of that process. The DUP input to the UK's approach to Brexit is highly constrained. The party has not sought to influence the broader UK position on Brexit, trusting the British government to deliver an exit that will be appropriate to Northern Ireland's best

---

8. The SEUPB is responsible to the Department of Finance in Northern Ireland and the Department of Public Expenditure and Reform in the Republic of Ireland along with the European Commission and the NSMC.

interests. The only other Northern Ireland MP who sits in parliament, the Independent Lady Sylvia Hermon, has vowed not to support the bill unless it is heavily amended. Because Sinn Féin refuses to take its seats in Westminster, and given the absence of SDLP MPs, there has been no nationalist representation in Westminster since the 2017 general election, so Northern Ireland's input to the debate on the bill is relatively insignificant. Compounded by the suspension of the Assembly and Executive, Northern Ireland representatives are effectively eliminated from all political fora for engagement. Rebalancing powers between the Northern Ireland Assembly and the UK parliament constitutes an issue of major political consequence. It potentially impinges on Northern Ireland's ability to maintain responsibility for all those areas with an EU dimension where it currently exercises devolved power.[9] The UK government has committed to restoring many, but possibly not all of these devolved powers to the regions. For some areas, possibly agriculture, central government may preserve some power in order to be able to pursue free trade deals. APNI Brexit Spokesperson, Stephen Farry (2017), has pointed out:

> A number of political parties, including Alliance, alongside a range of stakeholders have called for a special deal or set of arrangements for Northern Ireland, or even a special status. The content of what this means varies in practice, but one key element could be the prospect of Northern Ireland remaining as part of the European Single Market. In turn, this would entail full adherence to the Four Fundamental Freedoms in terms of the freedom of movement for goods, services, capital and labour. In order to make this happen, the Assembly would need to have full control over the regulatory levels to remain in compliance with EU law, the Acquis Communautaire.

The Withdrawal Bill may threaten Northern Ireland's ability to activate and operationalize a "special deal". None of these issues, however, are aired in either Westminster or Stormont. Northern Ireland's MPs are sanguine on this issue of potentially enormous significance for the

---

9. In Northern Ireland, there are 140 areas where EU law and devolved competences intersect (see Paun 2017).

future of devolved power in Northern Ireland. For unionists however, the prospect of the loss of devolved powers to the UK centre may be less problematic. In the first instance, it dents the possibility of special status being introduced and it also fits more broadly with unionist political affinities. MLAs may be more exercised by the issue, but with the absence of the Northern Ireland Assembly, there is no forum for the expression of opposition.

Northern Ireland has also been excluded from contributing to the wider parliamentary examination of the various dimensions to Brexit. A case in point is the House of Lords European Union Committee, which looked at the impact of Brexit on the UK's devolution settlements and was published in July 2017. Owing to the suspension of devolution in Northern Ireland and the upcoming Assembly elections in March 2017, it was not possible for the committee to take evidence from the Northern Ireland Executive or from party leaders. Instead, the committee consulted a former first minister and deputy first minister, representatives of the DUP and SDLP, a former secretary of state and an academic expert. The committee also visited Edinburgh and Cardiff during the course of their deliberations, but there was no such visit to Belfast. The lack of engagement with devolved powers in Northern Ireland, however, did not prevent the committee from noting that Northern Ireland "will be profoundly affected by Brexit" (House of Lords European Union Committee 2017: 24).

Representing more than the Republic of Ireland? The Irish government's approach to Brexit

The Irish government's early concerns about a possible Brexit were first contained in the 2014 *National Risk Assessment* (Department of the Taoiseach 2014: 17):

> A withdrawal of the UK from the European Union, or a period of continuing uncertainty regarding the UK's relationship with the EU would present significant challenges for Ireland in terms of (i) pursuit of Ireland's objectives as a Member State; (ii) bilateral relations with the UK including the economic and trading relationship; (iii) Northern Ireland issues.

The UK decision to leave the EU two years later dealt a considerable blow to Irish national interests. There are acute economic concerns about the potentially detrimental effect of the UK being outside the single market and the customs union. The erection of trade barriers between the Republic of Ireland and the UK poses fundamental risks for the Irish economy, while the effects of Brexit on the future of the CTA are equally problematic. At the EU level, the UK was always an important ally for Ireland at the negotiating table. The two states share similar perspectives on key EU policies and the loss of support on these issues leaves the Republic of Ireland vulnerable. There are fears too that the amelioration of British–Irish relations over recent years has been compromised by Brexit, as the two states embark on very different futures. Perhaps most significant, however, has been the Irish government's keen awareness of how Brexit has the potential to impact, politically and economically, on Northern Ireland. Where the British government was apparently less concerned (or possibly less aware) of the consequences of Brexit for Northern Ireland, the same cannot be said for the Irish government. In a speech at Queen's University Belfast in November 2015, the then Irish Foreign Affairs Minister, Charlie Flanagan, spoke about the uncertain impact of a UK vote to leave the EU on the status of the Irish border, and on the Irish and Northern Ireland economy. The minister also advised: "we must be wary of anything that has the potential – inadvertently or otherwise – to undo the progress that has been achieved over the last 30 years". The Irish government was visible and vocal during the EU referendum. The Taoiseach (and former Taoisigh), government ministers and senior diplomats (including former diplomats) were extensively mobilized during the referendum campaign. They met with their UK counterparts, delivered speeches, wrote opinion pieces, contributed to conferences and seminars, engaged with the Irish community across Britain, and used North–South institutions and bilateral contacts with the Northern Ireland administration to convey Ireland's position on key Brexit issues. The Department of the Taoiseach was restructured to facilitate a more focused approach to British–Irish relations in the context of the EU referendum, and other government departments were charged with identifying key strategic and sectoral issues for Ireland in the event of a Leave vote.[10]

---

10. The then Taoiseach Enda Kenny outlined the Irish government's activities during a statement to Dáil Éireann on UK/EU affairs on 21 April 2016.

Contingency planning for Brexit in Ireland

In the context of the various political, economic, institutional, cultural, social and familial links that exist between Northern Ireland and the Republic of Ireland (many of which are detailed in the 1998 Belfast Agreement), the latter has a legitimate interest to argue for minimizing the worst effects of Brexit on the Republic of Ireland and Northern Ireland. The Irish administration has, effectively, been fighting the Irish case, which has simultaneously entailed a strong defence of Northern Ireland interests. Following the referendum result, the Irish government shifted gears and moved to intensify the process of communicating and defending Irish interests at the EU level. This included more than a singular emphasis on promoting Irish economic interests. In a statement to the recalled Dáil Éireann three days after the EU referendum, then Taoiseach Enda Kenny stated: "Above all, our contingency management arrangements will prioritize the key political and strategic issues arising from the implications for Northern Ireland, the common travel area and the border".

From that point, the Irish government's 130 page Contingency Plan[11] became the centre-piece of Ireland's Brexit strategy. According to a senior Irish official, the Irish approach to Brexit is based on a four-fold strategy:

1. Intensive engagement with the EU and EU member states.
2. Contact and consultation with Northern Ireland.
3. Bilateral engagement with the UK.
4. Mitigating effects of Brexit at the domestic level (for example, by using budgetary measures to "Brexit-proof" the economy).

Consultation between the Irish government and Brexit stakeholders

Engaging with civil society and stakeholders has also been a central component of the Irish government's approach. The government created an

---

11. The Contingency Plan was kept confidential but a condensed version was made available to the media (see https://www.taoiseach.gov.ie/eng/News/Government_Press_Releases/Irish_Government_Brexit_Contingency_Plans_Announced.html, accessed 2 February 2018).

All-Island Civic Dialogue on Brexit, a participative and consultative exercise that aimed "to hear directly about the all-island implications of Brexit, from a variety of stakeholders and across a wide range of sectors". The government convened three plenary dialogues and over 20 sectoral dialogues during the first year of the Civic Dialogue. The plenary sessions typically involved inputs from the Taoiseach and government ministers. They included contributions from invited speakers, and breakout sessions to facilitate discussion around broad all-island Brexit topics. The sectoral dialogues had a narrower focus and cut across all government departments. A wide range of policies and issues were considered, including agri-food, energy, transport, tourism, further education and training, human rights and the Belfast Agreement, and the equine and greyhound sectors. There were up to 200 participants at each dialogue and they included representatives from organizations north and south of the border. The Northern Ireland participants included political parties, local councils, chambers of commerce, cross-border organizations, and interest groups. Unionist political parties, however, opted not to participate. DUP leader Arlene Foster denied the need for such an initiative, insisting that existing cross-border institutions were sufficient in terms of allowing for dialogue and discussion. The dialogues were, nevertheless, welcomed by a cross-section of civil society in both Northern Ireland and the Republic of Ireland, and supported by most Irish political parties.[12] A key positive for the Irish government in confronting the Brexit issue has been the level of cross-party support that has been forthcoming from opposition parties who have been broadly supportive of the Irish position and approach (although there is sporadic bickering).

Irish diplomacy and Brexit

The Irish government was consistently clear about its desire to see an orderly UK exit, and to achieve the closest possible relationship between the EU and the UK after Brexit, but equally the Irish government

---

12. A selection of All-Island Civic Dialogue participants share their perspectives on the value of the consultative and participative exercise: https://www.youtube.com/watch?v=_n5KC0YG0b8 (accessed 2 February 2018).

demonstrated realism about the challenges inherent in achieving this type of arrangement. In that context, the government worked particularly hard to shape the broader EU negotiating landscape. A significant development was the government's success at the 29 April 2017 EU summit in achieving an EU declaration recognizing the potential for Irish unification. The declaration (or "united Ireland clause") would allow Northern Ireland automatic membership of the EU in the event of unification. One commentator characterized this as a "stunning diplomatic coup" (Collins, 2017), which was won on the back of an extraordinary diplomatic effort by the Taoiseach, government ministers and officials. According to a former Irish government minister, the British government was opposed to the provision, but unable to prevent its inclusion.

The installation of new Taoiseach Leo Varadkar in June 2017 signalled something of a shift in the tenor and tone of the Irish government's approach to Brexit. There was clear frustration with the apparent British failure to appreciate the difficulties and sensitivities that Brexit poses on the island of Ireland, and there was also exasperation with the slow pace of progress during the first phase of negotiations. The Irish government was also irked by British government tactics, which were construed as being an attempt to force the EU (as opposed to the UK itself) to come up with proposals for the border. In a strongly worded rebuke, Taoiseach Varadkar adopted a harder diplomatic stance. He stated (Doyle 2017):

> We do not think it's in the interests of Northern Ireland or the United Kingdom that there should be an economic Border between our two countries or on our island and we're not going to be helping them to design some sort of Border that we don't believe should exist in the first place.

Unionists did not welcome the Taoiseach's intervention and accused him of engaging in unhelpful megaphone diplomacy. The Irish government was mildly enthusiastic about the UK *Position Paper on Northern Ireland and Ireland*. Foreign Minister Simon Coveney welcomed references to a "customs union partnership" and the British government's intention to seek border management options that were not reliant on physical and/or technological infrastructure (although this was not a firm commitment). The minister noted, however, a lack of detail about how the UK proposals might work and he expressed concerns about Ireland being used as a pawn in Brexit negotiations. The Irish reaction to the document hinted at tensions in relation to the British approach to the negotiations and frustration at the limited detail contained in the position paper.

Despite the slow emergence of concrete proposals from the UK, the Irish government recorded some successes in its ambitions to limit the impact of Brexit. References to Ireland and Northern Ireland have been influenced by Irish government efforts and ultimately, they have had some impact on how the UK has approached Brexit in the context of the British–Irish relationship. Specific Irish objectives have found expression in UK documents and papers, and the government's diplomatic and political efforts appear to have paid some dividends. There has also been strong EU acknowledgement of how Brexit impacts on both parts of the island of Ireland and this too has been important in terms of framing the overall Brexit negotiations.

Protecting the integrity of the European project: The EU's approach to Brexit

Throughout the period of UK and Irish membership of the EU, the EU has maintained an interest in Northern Ireland affairs. The EU "peace investment" in Northern Ireland has been subtle, but it has nevertheless been a part of the Union's broad and evolving conflict resolution capacity (see Stefanova 2011). There is some belief, therefore, that the EU has a political stake (albeit a small one) in seeing the Northern Ireland peace process secured. There is, however, a dilemma for the EU. Protecting the integrity of the Union is paramount during the Brexit negotiations. This is the primary objective for negotiators and it overrides all other considerations. Ireland is attuned to the possibility that if the EU adopts a hard-line approach to negotiations, Irish (and Northern Ireland) interests may well be a casualty. The EU is facing many challenges that potentially threaten its very existence. Electoral contests across EU member states and regional agitation across some member states (most especially Catalonia in Spain) have signalled increasing support for populist and Eurosceptic political parties and movements. Keeping a lid on the forces of disintegration is the primary concern of the EU. If ensuring this should require adopting a tough stance in relation to a departing member state, this may well be deemed a move worth taking.[13]

During the early stages of the Brexit negotiation period, the EU has been true to its longer-term support for Northern Ireland, and has also demonstrated a certain loyalty to the Republic of Ireland. Issues of concern to the Irish government and issues that impact on Northern Ireland have been expressly prioritized. Ireland/Northern Ireland was one of three EU priorities addressed during the first phase of the Brexit negotiations (alongside citizens' rights and financial liabilities), and the island of Ireland again formed a strand during the second phase of negotiations. The European Council elaborated on this in its guidelines for the Brexit negotiations (European Council 2017: paragraph 11):

> The Union has consistently supported the goal of peace and reconciliation enshrined in the Good Friday Agreement in all its parts, and continuing to support and protect the achievements, benefits and commitments of the Peace Process will remain of paramount importance.

The guidelines go on to emphasize and legitimize the need for "flexible and imaginative solutions" for avoiding a hard border on the island of Ireland. A European Parliament Resolution (2017/2593(RSP)) issued after Article 50 was triggered echoed these themes. The resolution:

> urges that all means and measures consistent with European Union law and the 1998 Good Friday Agreement be used to mitigate the effects of the United Kingdom's withdrawal on the border between Ireland and Northern Ireland; insists in that context on the absolute need to ensure continuity and stability of the Northern Ireland peace process and to do everything possible to avoid a hardening of the border.

---

13. During the economic crisis, Ireland bore the brunt of an EU decision to not write down sovereign debt, an action that came with very severe consequences not just for the Irish state, but for Irish citizens too. To some extent, that decision demonstrated the limits to EU support, a repeat of which cannot be ruled out.

The EU's commitment to limiting the impact of Brexit on Ireland/ Northern Ireland was further reiterated in an address to the Joint Houses of the Irish Oireachtas (parliament) in May 2017, Chief EU Brexit Negotiator, Michel Barnier, said: "I want to reassure the Irish people: in this negotiation Ireland's interest will be the Union's interest. We are in this negotiation together and a united EU will be here for you."

Barnier has some familiarity with Northern Ireland. He was European Commissioner with responsibility for the EU's Peace programme, and has an understanding of Northern Ireland's political situation. According to Ireland's EU Commissioner, Phil Hogan, Barnier understands "the nuance of what the political dimension is to the fragility of the peace [in Northern Ireland]" (Connolly 2017a: 62).[14] This was clearly reflected in his address to the Irish Oireachtas, which showed an appreciation of the many complex issues that Brexit poses for the island of Ireland. A very similar message is contained in the EU's *Guiding Principles for the Dialogue on Ireland/Northern Ireland* published later in 2017 by the European Commission. The document emphasizes the need to protect "the gains of the peace process and of the Good Friday Agreement (Belfast Agreement) in all its parts" (2). Like the Irish government, the EU has been resolute in placing the onus on the UK to propose solutions to the border issue. Also similar to Ireland, the EU has demonstrated some frustration with the UK's approach to the Brexit process. The EU response to the British government's *Position Paper on Northern Ireland and Ireland* was less restrained than that of Guy Verhofstadt MEP, who commented in a tweet: "To be in & out of the customs union & 'invisible borders' is a fantasy. First need to secure citizens' rights & a financial settlement." Michel Barnier's response was more measured and diplomatic, but it effectively conveyed the same message.

The EU's approach to dealing with the Irish border issue has demonstrated a willingness to consider bespoke proposals for Northern Ireland. The European Commission does not explicitly advocate or call for "special status" for Northern Ireland, but the possibility of facilitating

---

14. Michel Barnier is also a member of the EPP, of which Fine Gael are also members. He has a close relationship with former Taoiseach Enda Kenny and other party figures.

such a preference is implied. The frequent references to "flexible and imaginative solutions" enable consideration of special/unique proposals. Senior European Commission sources have claimed privately that a "standalone" deal on the border issue may be necessary (*The Guardian*, 1 September 2017). The European Commission's *Guiding Principles for the Dialogue on Ireland/Northern Ireland* also point to such a possibility. The document notes: "These challenges will require a unique solution which cannot serve to preconfigure solutions in the context of the wider discussions on the future relationship between the European Union and the United Kingdom".

The EP, however, has been somewhat less enthusiastic in advocating for special arrangements for Northern Ireland. The parliament rejected the amendment to the motion for a resolution on the Commission work programme. Amendment No. 38 tabled by the GUE/NGL read:

> Notes and respects the fact that the people of the *north of Ireland* and Scotland voted to remain in the EU; believes that an accommodation should be found whereby the *north of Ireland* maintains its membership of the European Union by whatever arrangement is necessary; calls on the EU to continue proactively to support the peace process in Ireland and to provide for its continuation in any negotiations on British withdrawal. (emphasis added)

Sinn Féin MEPs are members of the left-wing GUE/NGL political grouping. The amendment was roundly rejected by 374 votes to 66. The reluctance of MEPs to take a position on a live Brexit negotiating issue partially explains the depth of opposition. A further explanation relates to the wording of the amendment, which references the "north of Ireland" rather than Northern Ireland. During the debate, the UUP MEP Jim Nicolson objected to the reference noting that there is no such entity as the "north of Ireland", and so support for a proposal based on this wording may have been construed as the EP taking a position on the issue of identity in Northern Ireland. A well-placed EP source has pointed out that the vote should not necessarily be seen as the parliament taking a position against special status, rather: "It simply implies that the parliament does not want to take a position at this stage" (McBride, 6 July 2017).

The combination of these statements and positions suggests strong acknowledgement and awareness of specific Irish and Northern Ireland issues at the EU level, and considerable resolve in protecting those interests. Like the Republic of Ireland, however, the EU has encountered frustration with the pace and detail of the negotiations with the UK. Efforts to facilitate Northern Ireland interests are currently in evidence, but the extent to which these are sustainable in the longer term is unclear. The protection of the integrity of the EU will be a red line issue for the EU. Moreover, if Northern Ireland cannot assert boldly and loudly a strong position, the best interests of the region may be unclear, and possibly even overlooked.

Conclusion

The UK's withdrawal from the EU drew many responses, positions and strategies from those impacted by the decision. For the EU, the maintenance of the integrity of the Union is sacrosanct. For the Republic of Ireland, mitigating the worst effects of Brexit for the domestic economy, and for Northern Ireland is paramount. For the UK, Brexit implies a full exit from the EU. In Northern Ireland, Brexit became intermingled with the constitutional issue. There was no political unity, and parties pushed opposing remedies for the region's future after Brexit. Amidst this mix of divergent positions and seemingly incompatible preferences, is there scope for Northern Ireland interests to be accommodated in ways that ensure stability and are acceptable to all? There are two acute obstacles here that make agreement and accommodation especially difficult. The first is the absence of a functioning Executive and Assembly, and the second is the politicization of Brexit. The first obstacle removes a forum wherein some form of cross-party dialogue (if not agreement) might be achieved. The second makes for a toxic political environment that limits the extent to which constructive cross-party dialogue is even possible. And both of these obstacles are set against the challenging backdrop of a "negative peace".

The bulk of the Brexit debate and much of the negotiating process has been left to the British government and the European Commission with input from the Irish government. Key economic and political issues affecting Northern Ireland have received an airing, and there appeared an apparent willingness to prioritize those concerns. However, pressure to protect these interests was primarily communicated and pushed by non-Northern Ireland actors. Northern Ireland itself occupied the margins of the debate, and primarily so because of a lack of agreement between political parties as to how the process of achieving the softest possible Brexit can be framed and implemented. And yet, cross-community cooperation between parties is the most effective means of ensuring the articulation and protection of Northern Ireland political and economic interests at this precarious time. Irish Foreign Affairs Minister Simon Coveney (2017) has alluded to this: "An enhanced Northern Ireland voice articulating an agreed devolved government position could see more effective and inclusive representation of the unique circumstances of Northern Ireland at Westminster".

However, such is the level of mistrust between political parties in Northern Ireland, agreement has been elusive. The net result of this environment was that a strong Northern Ireland voice was effectively absent from one of the most important and potentially transformative events in recent British history. In a rather prescient observation before the EU referendum, the House of Common's Northern Ireland Affairs Committee noted (2016: 14):

> Clearly negotiations cannot exclusively prioritize the interests of Northern Ireland to the detriment of other parts of the UK. But neither can UK-level interests be allowed to dominate the UK's bargaining position at the expense of Northern Ireland. In the event of a vote to leave the EU, it is imperative that Northern Ireland's economic priorities, such as gaining a good deal for agricultural and manufactured goods, are given due prominence by the UK Government in any subsequent negotiations. However, the likelihood of this cannot be guaranteed.

Greater Northern Ireland input to the Brexit process offered one means of allowing "due prominence" to be achieved. The polarization that Brexit produced, coupled with a "negative peace" environment, and complicated further by a fracture in British–Irish relations, inhibited any detailed, mature and constructive discussion of how Northern Ireland could itself propose a response to the "flexible and imaginative" possibilities offered by the EU. The next chapter identifies what options there are for Northern Ireland's future outside the EU. It analyses the factors that inhibit the region's ability to infiltrate and influence discussions about the future terms of the UK/Northern Ireland relationship with the EU. An examination of earlier political crises in Northern Ireland highlights ways of overcoming the most intractable and insurmountable political differences to (slowly and painstakingly) find resolutions that are broadly acceptable.

5

Europe and Northern Ireland's future

Northern Ireland has overcome centuries of a violent and troubled past. The 1998 Belfast Agreement was a defining moment in the achievement of relative peace in Northern Ireland. The journey towards a permanent and stable peace, based on community reconciliation and ultimately integration, is, however, still a work in progress. Lingering differences epitomize the challenges associated with a "negative peace" and they underline the absence of trust that continues to aggravate political and community relations. Such is the power of these forces that they led to the suspension of the Northern Ireland power-sharing institutions during a crucial period after the EU referendum and during the Brexit negotiation period. Public policy issues lay victim to this dysfunctional political arena: progress on health, education, infrastructure and other policies and projects was stalled, while the Stormont chamber remained empty during its suspension. But perhaps even more problematic was the political silence on Brexit that suspension facilitated. Regrettable and potentially devastating, age-old sectarian quarrels prevented the people of Northern Ireland from having a voice in Brexit negotiations and decisions, and this posed a fundamental challenge to the region's economic well-being and to peace and stability in Northern Ireland.

The process of the UK leaving the EU spans a two-year period from March 2017 to March 2019 and involves thrashing out both withdrawal terms and a new UK relationship with the EU. During the negotiations, the Irish issue has been a central priority. Finding agreement on this issue, and specifically the border question, proved especially challenging for negotiators. To some extent, the lack of clarity about the nature of the future UK–EU trading relationship inhibited the possibility of achieving early agreement. The determination that "sufficient progress" had been achieved during phase one of negotiations did not signify a resolution of the Irish issue, rather it meant that the full two-year negotiation period would involve continued discussion of how to prevent a hard border on the island of Ireland in the context of UK withdrawal.

A further difficulty in relation to Northern Ireland's post-Brexit future related to the various options for managing the border between the UK and the Republic of Ireland. In the event of a soft Brexit, there would be little necessity for a bespoke arrangement for Northern Ireland as the status quo would remain largely intact. However, the UK government's determination to pursue a hard Brexit and leave the SEM and customs union, meant that some sort of special arrangement for Northern Ireland was if not likely, at least possible. Opposing unionist and nationalist perspectives about the desirability of so-called "special status" for Northern Ireland opened up a rift between the two communities and deepened existing divisions. The question of how to deal with Northern Ireland's unique circumstances became highly politicized and polarizing. This chapter identifies what options were available to deal with Northern Ireland's specific situation and it analyses why reaching agreement on a single agreed position proved so difficult. The chapter concludes by proposing that, despite unionist objections, some embrace of "specialness", in the context of the UK withdrawal from the EU, may in fact be the most effective means of safeguarding the unity of the UK and realizing unionist preferences.

The UK Brexit options

There are a number of possibilities available to the UK in terms of how to frame a post-Brexit trading relationship with the EU. Table 5.1 provides a summary of different scenarios including a no deal Brexit, and options ranging from a soft to a hard Brexit. Given the consistent lack of clarity about what type of deal the UK government favours, it is difficult to predict which of these options is favourable and feasible for the UK government. The softer EEA type Brexit arrangement has been rejected by Prime Minister Theresa May. This was evident in her Lancaster House speech (17 January 2017) and Florence

Speech (22 September 2017), and in HM Government's (2017b) White Paper. Talk of a no deal Brexit and a UK exit from the EU that results in the imposition of WTO trading rules is undesirable, but the UK government has not excluded such a scenario. Some of the preferential models outlined in Table 5.1 can also be dismissed as they do not fit with the stated (if somewhat confusing and contradictory) preferences touted by the UK government. This points towards the Canadian model, the Comprehensive Economic and Trade Agreement (CETA), as being a possible template for a future EU–UK trading arrangement. Senior Conservative Party figures, including the Minister for Exiting the EU, David Davis, and Chief EU Brexit Negotiator Michel Barnier have all, at various times, alluded to a CETA-style arrangement.[1] Such an agreement would mean being outside the customs union and SEM, but the UK would enjoy tariff free trade with the EU and vice versa (although there would probably be exceptions for many products as is the case for Canada). Significantly, CETA does not remove non-tariff barriers, which means that obstacles to full free trade with the EU would exist. However, CETA does not oblige Canada to pay into the EU budget, or to sign up to the principles of free movement, or to abide by European Court of Justice (ECJ) rulings. Instead, any trade disputes are judged by a permanent tribunal body. This type of post-Brexit relationship with the EU does have certain attractions for a UK government that has been adamant in relation to ending UK budget contributions to the EU, withdrawing from the jurisdiction of the ECJ and reasserting national control over immigration. In this particular CETA-style scenario, however, there would be consequences for the management of the border on the island of Ireland, and this is the fundamental nub of the Brexit issue for both countries.

---

1. The UK Minister for Exiting the EU, David Davis, praised the CETA model in a speech before the EU referendum (see Davis 2016). Leading Brexiteer and Conservative Party grandee, Foreign Secretary Boris Johnson, has alluded to an EU–UK free trade arrangement akin to CETA (see Mason 2016). From an EU perspective, Chief Brexit Negotiator, Michel Barnier, noted: "From the moment the UK told us that it wants out of the single market and the customs union, we will have to work on a model that is closer to the agreement signed with Canada" (Boffey 2017).

Table 5.1 Summary of scenarios or models for the EU's agreements with other countries

Scenario	Assessment
1. EEA	Close to the status quo, too close for UK
1.1 EEA + customs union	Theoretical case, very close to status quo, too close for UK
2. WTO	Considerable lessening of market access, default regime for UK
2.1 + aggressive competition	With non-cooperative tax and regulatory competition
3. Preferential models	
3.1 Simple FTA (free trade area)	Possible, but UK wants a more ambitious "Comprehensive FTA"
3.2 Customs union (with FTA)	More than simple FTA, but UK does not want customs union
3.3 Swiss model	Selective and flexible in the past, but not available for the UK
3.4 CETA (Canada)	Comprehensive, beyond simple FTA; no EU acquis content
3.5 DCFTA (Ukraine)	Deep and Comprehensive, with much EU acquis content
3.6 SAA (Balkans)	Weaker than DCFTA, for accession candidates, not for UK
3.7 PCA (Kazakhstan)	Little more than WTO, not for UK
3.8 Strategic Partnership	Summit level global diplomacy
3.9 Strategic Partnership with CFTA	= UK objective (i.e. a Comprehensive FTA, somewhere between CETA and DCFTA?)

Source: European Parliament (2017: 26).

A CETA-type arrangement lends itself to harder borders because it requires customs controls to enforce rules of origin,[2] to prevent smuggling, to ensure traceability for VAT, and more. In other words, a CETA

---

2. The customs union regime applies a common customs duty to goods that are imported from outside the EU. However, many imported goods are manufactured in more than one country. The EU has created rules for establishing the country of origin of imported and exported goods (that is rules of origin). This allows traders to determine which goods may qualify for preferential treatment under the terms of the applicable free trade area or free trade agreement between the EU and a third country. Should the UK enter into a CETA-style agreement with the EU, it will be outside the EU customs union and so customs controls will be required to enforce rules of origin.

scenario is not compatible with the notion of "seamless and friction-less borders" as espoused by the UK government. This means that the frontier between the UK and the Republic of Ireland will require the imposition of border control measures, which would pose pro-found choices and challenges for Northern Ireland. First, to what extent can such border management arrangements between the UK and the Republic of Ireland be soft, seamless, frictionless, invisible? Second, *where* should those border arrangements be located? Currently, the possibilities include: at or away from the land frontier; in the Irish Sea; or around the two islands of Ireland and Britain. All of these options pose their own set of financial and logistical difficulties, but it is their economic and political ramifications that present the most challeng-ing and complex predicaments for the Brexit negotiators. Because the British government has been slow to clarify what form of Brexit it favours, this has necessarily meant some difficulty in expressing a preference about how the Irish border issue might be addressed. The problem is equally evident in Northern Ireland, where unionists and nationalists have failed to agree a common Brexit preference.

The Northern Ireland Brexit options

For Northern Ireland, the least disruptive Brexit deal, one that allows for the land border between the UK and Ireland to remain largely as it is, would see the UK remaining in the Customs Union and SEM. This scenario, however, has been ruled out by Prime Minister Theresa May. Short of this option, the EU has made it clear that tailored arrange-ments would be considered to ease Brexit-induced economic and political pressures on Northern Ireland. So, what are the options? Unionists and nationalists have very different conceptions of the options that are available to safeguard a soft border arrangement.

Nationalism and "special status"

There are a raft of special arrangements that accommodate the interests of various overseas territories with links to EU member states. In total, there are 25 such territories that have special relationships with the

EU.[3] The arrangements for the overseas territories demonstrate that different forms of accommodation are possible under the auspices of EU law. Crucially however, the special status that Northern Ireland nationalists advocate for would be markedly different in that the region would remain (fully or partially) inside the EU while the rest of the UK would be outside.[4] There is no precedent or template for such an arrangement. The idea of territorial differentiation, however, has been proposed as a means of acknowledging and accommodating Northern Ireland's specific interests (see Doherty *et al.* 2017; Phinnemore & Hayward 2017).

The nationalist bloc, comprising Sinn Féin and the SDLP, has pushed for a form of special or unique status for Northern Ireland that is based on the notion of territorial differentiation. The essence of such an arrangement would facilitate the continuation of the free movement of trade and people on the island of Ireland. The parties have similar views on what constitutes special status (see Table 5.2), but in essence the arrangement would mean the continuation of free movement of trade and people across the Irish land border.

In terms of the practicalities of securing special status for Northern Ireland, the devil is in the detail and that detail is not fully developed in either the Sinn Féin or SDLP proposals. In order for Northern Ireland to continue to have access to the SEM when the rest of the UK does not, customs and immigration checks would have to be located away from the land border and instead be placed at ports and airports. In practice, this would mean a (sort of) barrier between Northern Ireland and the rest of the UK. It is important to note that the question of a post-Brexit border in the Irish Sea largely applies only to trade.[5] The SDLP (2017: 2)

---

3. The territorial status of EU countries and certain territories is detailed on the European Commission website (see https://ec.europa.eu/taxation_customs/business/vat/eu-vat-rules-topic/territorial-status-eu-countries-certain-territories_en, accessed 2 February 2018).

4. In the case of EU overseas territories, the countries to which they are linked are member states of the EU.

5. Katy Hayward (2017b) notes that this is so because both the Republic of Ireland and the UK are not members of the Schengen Zone of free movement. EU citizenship rights will also be decided separately: "The UK and Ireland both need to pass legislation in order to guarantee the rights of Irish and British citizens in their respective territories if these rights are to continue to stand above those of EU citizens. How British and Irish citizens are distinguished from others within the UK after Brexit will entail other procedures that are not found at the physical border."

Table 5.2 SDLP and Sinn Féin proposals for special status for Northern Ireland

Issue	SDLP	Sinn Féin
SEM	Membership of SEM	Access to SEM
EU funding	Continued participation in EU funding and programmes (including CAP)	Maintenance of all EU funding streams (including CAP)
CTA and all-island economy	Measures to ensure further development of the all-island economy, by building on the CTA	Remain part of the CTA
Workers' rights	Protection of rights of cross-border workers	Protection of access to employment, workers' rights and working conditions
Political representation	Securing all-island representation in the European Parliament and on other EU bodies	Northern Ireland Executive Ministers occasionally attend Council of Ministers meetings; additional seats for Ireland in European Parliament and other EU bodies
Human rights	Securing of human rights and protections derived from EU law	Protection of the peace process, including human rights guarantees
Environment	Avoid "race to the bottom" as regards environmental standards and social provisions	Maintenance of EU environmental protections, including EU energy law as it applies to the all-island electricity market

document states: "We have been clear that if any border is to emerge as a result of this referendum, it must be around the island of Ireland, and not across it". For unionism, such an arrangement is highly problematic as it would differentiate Northern Ireland from the rest of the UK. The fundamental basis for unionism is its attachment and allegiance to the UK, so any processes or measures that chip away at existing links are deemed to threaten the Union and to be an attack on unionism itself. The intention of special status is also viewed with deep suspicion by unionists. UUP leader, Robert Swann has labelled special status as "a united Ireland by the back door" (McAleese 2017). This interpretation and conception of special status is viewed as a step along the road towards removing Northern Ireland permanently from the UK. In other words, special status is equated with an assault on core unionist principles and preferences. From the unionist perspective, it poses a menacing constitutional threat, which explains their ardent opposition to nationalist proposals for special status.

For nationalists, the benefits of special status are couched in terms of protecting Northern Ireland's peace process, and also respecting the terms of the Belfast Agreement that provide nationalists with important political, institutional, cultural and identity safeguards. For Sinn Féin (2016: 2): "Brexit undermines the institutional, constitutional and legal integrity of the Good Friday Agreement". Former Prime Minister Tony Blair, one of the architects of the Agreement, has stated that it was written and agreed on the assumption of both Irish and UK membership of the EU (Gilmore 2017): "Brexit raises uncertain implications for many of the key issues addressed by the GFA [Good Friday Agreement], including those of identity, equality, parity of esteem and the health of the cross-border and bilateral relationships".

Many of these features of the Agreement relate to nationalist sensibilities in relation to identification with the rest of Ireland through the right to Irish (and thus EU) citizenship, and through all-island bodies such as the NSMC and sectoral Implementation Bodies. Brexit, however, challenges the spirit and the functioning of the Agreement by undermining legal certainty, jeopardizing the operation of cross-border institutions, and changing the UK's constitutional status as a member of the EU. If Northern Ireland is to move outside the EU, there will be a necessity to revise elements of the (hard-fought) Agreement to reflect a new Brexit reality. In addition, the revised document may need to be put to the electorates in the Republic of Ireland and Northern Ireland (as was the case in 1998) (see Tonge 2017b). Revising the document and holding a referendum pose their own set of acute challenges for Northern Ireland parties and voters, and would probably stoke old tensions and arguments. Moreover, the prospect of agreeing new wording and ensuring its support in a plebiscite is arguably even more challenging. The SDLP shares the Sinn Féin perspective as to the impact of Brexit on the Belfast Agreement. The party has also proposed that as part of any special status, North–South bodies should be recast: "This would include both a realignment of thematic areas and an intensification of existing work" (SDLP 2017: 6). The SDLP response to Brexit, therefore, proposes not just protecting existing cross-border arrangements, but strengthening them further.

For nationalists, there is more to special status than just its political ramifications for the Belfast Agreement and the peace process. It is also viewed as being more economically advantageous for Northern Ireland because it maintains access to the SEM, which is Northern Ireland's largest market. Over half of Northern Ireland exports go to the EU. In this context (Northern Ireland Assembly Research and Information Service 2016a: 9): "Northern Ireland is more reliant on the EU as an export market than the UK as a whole [is] and ... the region could be more exposed should this market access be restricted in the event of the UK exiting the EU".

The proposed economic upside of special status is to the benefit of all of Northern Ireland – unionists and nationalists alike. Unionists, however, dispute this argument. As Northern Ireland does more business with the rest of the UK than with the Republic of Ireland, erecting an economic barrier between Northern Ireland and the rest of the UK would be economically detrimental. DUP MEP Diane Dodds notes: "We would not countenance and indeed it would be calamitous for the economy in Northern Ireland if there were barriers to trade with our largest partner which is the rest of the United Kingdom" (RTE News, 20 September 2017).

In essence, unionists and nationalists do not agree on the economic impact of Brexit (and special status) and this colours their views. Whereas nationalists equate special status with the promise of economic stability, unionists disagree. Northern Ireland nationalists, however, are not alone in favouring a special status Brexit arrangement. The APNI is also supportive:

> Alliance will continue to argue for special arrangements to be negotiated and put in place for Northern Ireland, and for this region to be accorded a Special Deal in terms of either continued associate membership of the European Union or a bespoke relationship with it.[6]

---

6. The APNI Brexit policy is available on the party website: https://www.allianceparty.org/page/brexit, accessed 2 February 2018.

In the Republic of Ireland, opposition parties including Fianna Fáil are seeking for Northern Ireland to be designated as "special status",[7] and the Irish Labour Party has been similarly vocal in supporting the SDLP (their sister party's) position on special status (see Labour Party 2017). A 2015 report by the Joint Oireachtas Committee on European Affairs made a similar proposal in relation to granting Northern Ireland a "special position" within the UK that would allow for the maintenance of North–South relations and Northern Irish EU citizenship rights. The Irish government has similarly hinted at its support for bespoke arrangements to cater to Northern Ireland interests. Minister for Foreign Affairs Simon Coveney stated: "What we are insisting on achieving is a special status for Northern Ireland that allows the interaction on this island, as is currently the case, to be maintained" (RTE News, 23 June 2017).[8] More recently however, the Irish government shied away from explicit references to special status. During a parliamentary exchange on 3 October 2017, Taoiseach Leo Varadkar stated:

> We have not proposed special economic status for the North because what we are proposing would not require it. Our proposition is that the trading relationship between the United Kingdom and Ireland should remain the same. I set out how this could be done in the speech I made in Belfast, first, in a long transition phase, second, through a customs union partnership which would still be a form of customs union between the United Kingdom and the European Union and also an EU–UK free trade area which would negate the need for a special zone.

The government was also reluctant to use the term "special status" during a two-day parliamentary debate on Brexit in September 2017. Ministers' failure to answer opposition questions on the subject of special status caused some frustration among opposition TDs. Minister Simon Coveney defended the government's approach: "I will

---

7. Fianna Fáil's Brexit policy is available on the party website: https://www.fiannafail.ie/brexit/, accessed 2 February 2018.
8. The Minister later clarified that he had in fact meant "unique status" rather than "special status".

not behave in [a] party political way on this issue. I hope that other Members will work with me in a constructive [manner] to try to find an outcome for Ireland that is workable in the context of a very complex environment".

Despite the Irish government's reticence to use the term, there is what might be termed strong pan-nationalist weight behind calls for special status. This became even more evident following the sixth round of Brexit negotiations in November 2017 when an EU working paper proposed that Northern Ireland remain within the customs union and single market. The document was drafted with the agreement of the Irish government. Widespread support among the broad nationalist family on both sides of the Irish border is not echoed by the British government or the unionist bloc in Northern Ireland. Indeed, such is the level of support for special status among nationalists that it has arguably heightened unionist opposition to any talk of special arrangements.

Unionism and "special status"

Unionist rejection of special status[9] for Northern Ireland has been emphatic and forthright. It has been ruled out consistently by all of the unionist political parties. Former UUP leader Lord Trimble dismissed the idea as "rubbish";[10] DUP MP Nigel Dodds labelled special status "a nonsense";[11] and TUV leader Jim Allister has called it a "trap".[12] This opposition is shared by some members of the Conservative Party

---

9. It should be noted that the term "special status" is problematic for unionists. During a House of Lords debate (27 February 2017), UUP peer Lord Empey explained: "The concept of special status has been mentioned. That term referred to the special category status of prisoners in the Maze prison – or Long Kesh, as it then was – which led to the hunger strike. 'Special status', certainly to a unionist, means something less than being part of the United Kingdom – and that is exactly what it would be."

10. Quoted in: "Paisley, Tebbit and Trimble all savage idea of Brexit border in the sea", *Newsletter*, 29 July 2017, available at: http://www.newsletter.co.uk/news/business/paisley-tebbit-and-trimble-all-savage-idea-of-brexit-border-in-the-sea-1-8078800, accessed 2 February 2018.

11. Quoted in: House of Lords European Union Committee (2017: 14).

12. "Special status – a ruse to break up the UK", *Statement by TUV Leader Jim Allister*, 3 April 2017, available at: http://tuv.org.uk/special-status-a-ruse-to-break-up-the-uk/, accessed 2 February 2018.

including Lord Tebbit, who also voiced opposition to special status for Northern Ireland. The British government has similarly aligned itself with the unionist position, although Westminster has been less blunt in its objections to special status. In its *Brexit: Devolution* report, the House of Lords European Union Committee states (2017: 25):

> "Special status" is a politically contentious term in Northern Ireland, and we acknowledge the unionist community's concerns that no aspect of the Brexit negotiations should undermine Northern Ireland's ties to the rest of the UK. Yet at the same time, the specific circumstances in Northern Ireland give rise to unique issues that will need to be addressed during the Brexit negotiations.

Despite fervent opposition to special status, unionists nevertheless acknowledge that in the context of Brexit, there are circumstances specific to Northern Ireland that demand special attention. DUP MP Sammy Wilson has noted that Northern Ireland would be affected by Brexit "in a different, or perhaps in a more concentrated, way" than other parts of the UK (House of Lords 2017: 19). His party colleague Nigel Dodds similarly accepts that "There are special circumstances in Northern Ireland and we will try to make sure these are recognised" (*The Guardian*, 9 June 2017). There are substantial difficulties, however, for unionism in terms of reconciling Northern Ireland's specific needs with the idea of special status and that is because "special status" has become conflated with the nationalist aspiration of a united Ireland. Unionists are particularly distrustful of Sinn Féin. UUP MLA Danny Kinahan is not alone in his belief that "Sinn Féin are attempting to use 'special status' as a guise to break up the Union" (UUP 2017a). In this way, the Brexit discussion is couched in terms of the age-old nationalist versus unionist quarrel about Northern Ireland's constitutional future. This has contributed to a toxic political environment that makes the challenge of forging agreement on Northern Ireland's post-Brexit future pointedly difficult.

In addition to being suspicious about nationalist motives *vis-à-vis* Brexit, unionists are concerned about the Irish government's approach to the EU negotiations. In her 2016 party conference speech, DUP leader Arlene Foster suggested that the Irish government was sabotaging Northern Ireland economic interests: "While they [the

Irish government] seek to take the views of people of Northern Ireland on the issue of Brexit at home, their representatives are sent out around the world to talk down our economy and to attempt to poach our investors".

A senior UUP figure also alluded to the Irish government being "disingenuous" in terms of its activities in Brussels, suggesting that, behind the scenes, it was negotiating in its own interests and to the detriment of Northern Ireland.

From the unionist perspective, there is an onus on the Irish government to be to the fore in finding a solution to the border issue. This is so because Brexit may be as damaging for the Republic of Ireland as it is for Northern Ireland. DUP MP Sir Jeffery Donaldson has noted (Moriarty 2017):

> We have to cooperate here. A solution has to be one that is agreed and that means Dublin has to have an input. If Dublin refuses to co-operate on this inevitably we are going to end up in a different arrangement that could result in some sort of hard border. Now that's not in Dublin's interests – the Irish economy would suffer greatly if we can't find an agreed way forward.

The Irish government, however, has categorically stated that it will not contribute to the design of a post-Brexit border. One senior Irish civil servant noted: "If we are designing, we are conceding". On the back of this logic, the Irish political apparatus is not contemplating, researching or drafting any plans for a border (of any sort) on the island of Ireland. A technological soft border has also been categorically ruled out by the Irish government. In a *Belfast Telegraph* op-ed, Minister Simon Coveney stated (17 August 2017):

> with such a serious issue [i.e. Brexit], it is important to be honest and clear – seeing technology as the answer misunderstands the problem. We cannot rely on technology alone to solve political questions. Cameras, checks, delays and the resulting possibility of increased security issues at the border would pose a major political challenge that would have serious implications for both governments, for the people of the island and for the peace process.

From an Irish government perspective, a political solution to the border issue is imperative. In this context, unionists have proposed an alternative to special status for Northern Ireland, but it is one that is anathema to nationalism and more especially, it is utterly unacceptable to the Irish government. UUP MEP Jim Nicholson notes that instead of special status for Northern Ireland: "What we need are innovative and bespoke arrangements for both the UK outside the European Union, and the Irish Republic within it" (UUP 2017b). Both unionist parties, however, have been vague in relation to what precisely they favour in terms of Northern Ireland's future post Brexit. The UUP's document, *A Vision for Northern Ireland Outside the EU* (2016b), outlines the party's opposition to a hard border at the land frontier, and at British ports and airports. This alludes to some sort of border around both the island of Ireland and the rest of the UK. A similar proposal was made more explicitly by DUP MP Ian Paisley Jnr (2017) who suggests: "the Republic should be seeking from the EU26 a special status for itself". The DUP MP suggested that if a hard border is erected on the island of Ireland, it will be the fault of the Irish government. He proceeded to urge the Republic of Ireland to consider leaving the EU along with the UK, arguing that such a move would go some way to safeguarding both Irish and Northern Ireland economic interests. Cross-bench peer and former UUP MEP Lord Kilclooney echoes this view (House of Lords debate, 27 February 2017):

> Of course, a special status is required for someone but not for Northern Ireland. It is offensive to suggest that it should have a special status. It is the Republic that needs it. We must keep the common travel area there, and we must get Brussels to recognise, as the Prime Minister of the Republic of Ireland has stated, that the Republic will be more seriously damaged than any other nation in the European Union. It will suffer badly. It is suffering already, but what will it be like in two and a half years' time when the United Kingdom leaves the European Union? The Republic of Ireland needs special status and we should support it in its attempts to get that in Brussels.

Irish officials and politicians are resolute in their opposition to such a proposal. Drawing a border around both the island of Ireland and the UK is viewed as akin to Ireland exiting the EU and there is no political appetite whatsoever in the Republic of Ireland for such a prospect. In his 2017 interview with *Time Magazine*, Taoiseach Leo Varadkar categorically ruled out the possibility of Ireland following the UK out of the EU: "It is something we are not even considering and something we can rule out" (Duggan 2017). He pointed to other examples when Ireland did not follow the UK example including, in an EU context, the Irish decision to join the single currency zone in 1999. The Taoiseach's views are backed up by senior civil servants who are clear that: "there is no question of an Ir-exit". These positions are supported by public opinion survey data that demonstrates exceptionally strong support for Irish membership of the EU. An EM Ireland/Red C poll published in May 2017 found that 88 per cent of Irish people agreed that Ireland should remain a part of the EU.

Unionism is seeking to alter the way in which Brexit is currently depicted as a British problem by suggesting that it is equally, if not more so, a problem for the Republic of Ireland too. Neither nationalists nor the Irish government are receptive to this interpretation of the Brexit challenge and therein lies a serious difficulty for both sides. There is, in effect, a fundamental mismatch between unionism and nationalism as to how the same outcome, that is no physical border on the island of Ireland, might be reached.

The Brexit possibilities

The UK's future relationship with the EU is uncertain. A soft Brexit has been all but ruled out, although it cannot be definitively discounted – a change of UK government, for example, may produce a new Brexit dynamic. However, Prime Minister Theresa May has been reasonably consistent in proposing a hard Brexit, perhaps along the lines of the CETA arrangement. There is also, however, an albeit slimmer possibility of a no Brexit deal. Hardline Tory Brexiteers have voiced support for such an option if the negotiations do not bend to core UK demands. What would each of these scenarios mean for Northern Ireland? Three possible scenarios are likely:

1. No Brexit Deal
2. Hard Brexit
3. (Hard) Brexit with Special Deal for Northern Ireland

Scenarios 1 and 2 would entail the reinstallation of a physical international border between Northern Ireland and the Republic of Ireland. This would come with substantial economic and political costs (see Chapter 3). There may also be diplomatic costs in terms of a further fracturing of the UK–Ireland relationship. From a constitutional perspective, there are two possible reactions to these scenarios. First, the severe economic consequences for the Irish economy may force some contemplation of an Ir-exit. Greater public unease with the EU resulting from a harsher economic environment may increase support for Eurosceptic forces. Those forces may leverage public dissatisfaction and push more rigorously for Ireland to leave the EU. The extent to which this may produce an elevated appetite for an Ir-exit, however, is unclear. Given the very high levels of public support for the EU in the Republic of Ireland, and given that the Irish government is politically committed to EU membership, such an outcome appears highly unlikely.

A second, and more likely response to a hard Brexit is to be found in Northern Ireland. Should the severity of a Brexit-related economic downturn be intense, it would pose severe difficulties for all sections and sectors of society in Northern Ireland. Emboldened by a situation not of Northern Ireland's making, and yet detrimental to its economic well-being, nationalist support for a united Ireland is likely to grow, possibly to the point where a border poll becomes inevitable.[13] Nationalist logic would be buttressed by the united Ireland clause agreed between the EU and the Republic of Ireland in advance of the start of Brexit negotiations, which would effectively guarantee Northern Ireland membership of the EU in the event of Irish unity. However, any referendum on Irish unity in Northern Ireland would be a politically charged and divisive episode that may prompt instability, a resurgence of communal tensions and at worst lead to a return to violence. A referendum that returned support for a united Ireland would also create constitutional upheaval across the UK by fracturing the unity

---

13. According to the 1998 Belfast Agreement, a border poll can only be triggered when there is evidence to suggest that a referendum on Irish unity is likely to succeed. Schedule 1 of the 1998 Agreement states: "the Secretary of State shall exercise the power under paragraph 1 if at any time it appears likely to him that a majority of those voting would express a wish that Northern Ireland should cease to be part of the United Kingdom and form part of a united Ireland".

of the United Kingdom and undermining the broader constitutional settlement. The Scottish independence movement may derive inspiration from Northern Ireland and seek a similar referendum leading to Scotland also exiting the UK. The break-up of the UK would become a reality and its political, constitutional and economic future would be profoundly impacted. The reality of a united Ireland would also pose challenges for the Republic of Ireland. Unification would entail political and financial costs, and would require some restructuring to accommodate Northern Ireland citizens, interests and political parties. The Joint Oireachtas Committee on the Implementation of the Good Friday Agreement has advocated preparing for such a scenario. The committee's report *Brexit and the Future of Ireland: Uniting Ireland and Its People in Peace and Prosperity* proposes: "The establishment of a New Ireland Forum 2 is recommended to set a pathway to achieve the peaceful reunification of Ireland" (2017: 15). The report was ridiculed by unionists, but welcomed by nationalists. However, the publication of such a document signals that the subject (and possibility) of Irish unity is on the political agenda in the Republic of Ireland and there are few signs that this constitutional genie will be put back in the bottle. The EU may also face challenges should a united Ireland become a reality. There is a keenness at the EU level to dampen nationalist/separatist sentiment because anything that fuels national constitutional turmoil (note the constitutional crisis in Catalonia and Spain) is potentially destabilizing for the EU. The dangers of a hard Brexit or a no Brexit deal are potentially far-reaching, not just for Northern Ireland but for the UK, the Republic of Ireland and the EU too.

Scenario 3, a special Brexit deal for Northern Ireland, is possible, but highly contentious. The prospect of special status for Northern Ireland exposes a serious rift between the two political blocs in Northern Ireland. Nationalists support it, unionists vehemently oppose it. Their support and opposition are fuelled by both political and economic motives. Nationalists seek to keep Northern Ireland within the customs union and SEM, while unionists wish to preserve unfettered trade links with the rest of the UK. Nationalists wish to maintain (and strengthen) existing cross-border links and institutions, while unionists interpret this as a slow march towards a united Ireland. For nationalists, the perceived benefits of special status are clear. For unionists, there is little to recommend such a status. However, an important (and perhaps

under-appreciated) side-effect of special status is that it would probably simultaneously curtail calls for a border poll. The logic of a border
poll would be challenged by such an arrangement because special status would effectively secure the economic, political and constitutional
status quo on the island of Ireland. Despite unionist fears, the integrity of the current UK constitutional arrangement would in fact be
strengthened rather than weakened by special status. Unionism voiced
similar concerns about the potential for North–South institutions
agreed during the Belfast Agreement negotiations in 1998, to herald
moves towards a united Ireland. These institutional novelties, however,
have done little to advance the united Ireland agenda, rather they have
produced a pragmatic form of cross-border cooperation that is free of
any covert constitutional schema. Based on this analysis, the impact of
special status is unlikely to unleash the type of constitutional pressures
that unionism fears. Short of a UK-wide soft Brexit, the alternatives to
special status are potentially much more harmful to unionist aspirations than any proposal to grant Northern Ireland special status.

Of all the options available to the UK government in dealing with
Northern Ireland and Brexit, facilitating a new form of special status
for Northern Ireland following the UK exit from the EU may be the
more palatable and politically less contentious option. A special deal
for Northern Ireland would effectively (and perhaps counterintui-
tively) respond to some of the more serious concerns of nationalists *and*
unionists. Forcing or imposing such a scenario on Northern Ireland,
however, is not prudent as it risks further antagonizing an already
delicate and fragile "negative peace". There are, however, intense difficulties in achieving cross-communal consensus on a post-Brexit deal
for Northern Ireland.

Reaching consensus on Brexit in Northern Ireland

The starting point for developing a common Northern Ireland position
on Brexit pitches opposing parties against each other. The DUP and
TUV campaigned for Leave and in the aftermath of the vote, these parties along with the UUP support the UK exit from the EU. In contrast,
Sinn Féin, the SDLP and APNI supported Remain and favour finding a
means for Northern Ireland to remain in the customs union and single

market. These seemingly discordant preferences, however, may not be as stark as they may appear.

First, there is a wholesale understanding among Northern Ireland political parties that the UK is leaving the EU. In other words, there is consensus across the political divide that the UK is embarked on an exit route, and that Northern Ireland is on that path too. Political parties are effectively agreed on the final Brexit outcome. The detail of how that exit is achieved is where party positions begin to diverge. On the face of it however, and in terms of what the final Brexit outcome may look like for Northern Ireland specifically, the gap between the parties is less substantial than might be assumed.

A second important observation, therefore, relates to the political parties in Northern Ireland and their common perspectives in relation to achieving the softest possible Brexit. The only effort at articulating a joint Northern Ireland position was the first minister and deputy first minister's joint letter to the prime minister (August 2016) identifying the *outcomes* that both the DUP and Sinn Féin envisaged as being in Northern Ireland's best interests. Neither party wants to see a hard border on the island of Ireland or restrictions on the free movement of people, goods and services. The letter explicitly referenced the need for Northern Ireland to continue to have access to skilled and unskilled labour. The first minister and deputy first minister were also at one in wanting to safeguard the agri-business sector and to protect the integrated electricity market. The letter also stated: "It is equally important that the border does not create an incentive for those who would wish to undermine the peace process and/or the political settlement". Interestingly, the letter does not make explicit reference to the customs union or SEM, and it does not include ideas about "special status". Indeed, the document contains no details about *process*, but is instead focused on a Brexit *outcome* that is agreeable to both parties.

Many of the preferences detailed in the first minister and deputy first minister's letter are repeated in the DUP and Sinn Féin election manifestos, various policy documents and political pronouncements. Similar preferences are also discernible for other parties including the SDLP and UUP. The language and tone may be less measured, and the options for achieving a soft Brexit may differ, but nevertheless it is possible to identify common preferred outcomes that cut across the political divide.

Third, in any negotiation there are a number of parties. The Brexit negotiations are conducted between the UK government and the EU, specifically the European Commission's Brexit taskforce. The Irish government also has a stake in the Brexit negotiations, but is not at the negotiating table. Irish interests and preferences are being filtered through the EU negotiating team. Historically, and in the context of its ongoing support for the peace process, the EU has a record of facilitating tailored financial and practical support for Northern Ireland. This remains in evidence. The EU negotiating guidelines state that the EU is open to "flexible and imaginative solutions" in dealing with Brexit as it affects the island of Ireland, a message that has since been reiterated in various documents and by a number of senior EU figures. There is an openness to facilitating a form of Brexit that recognizes the specific circumstances that pertain in Northern Ireland, in terms of the CTA, cross-border cooperation and the border. The last of these issues is the most vexing, and it is the one where progress has been painstakingly difficult. The onus for proposing ways and means of preventing a hard border has been placed squarely with the British government. For its part, the British government has welcomed the EU's flexibility on the border issue, but the UK negotiating team has nevertheless been slow to identify creative ways of preventing a hard border. Sensitivity to Northern Ireland political interests limits the extent to which workable proposals can be furnished. There is currently no "solution" that is palatable to both unionists and nationalists. Both camps have very different views about the *process* of how to facilitate a soft border.

Fourth, the EU referendum result, in which 55.8 per cent of the Northern Ireland electorate opted for Remain, is an important context within which to frame Northern Ireland's Brexit position. Most of the electorate, albeit on a relatively low turnout, supported the UK remaining in the EU. The Remain vote included strong nationalist and some unionist support. In a similar vein, the Brexit vote mobilized a cross-section of civil society in Northern Ireland. The economic stakes were perceived to be high for many Northern Ireland business interests, and some organizations produced advanced positions on Brexit.[14]

---

14. In June 2017, in an open letter to the government, five of the UK's leading business organizations, the British Chambers of Commerce (BCC), the Confederation

For sectors like the agri-food and energy sectors (among others), the implications of Brexit are potentially very serious and have compelled extensive engagement.[15] The voluntary and community sector harbour deep concerns about the loss of EU funding, and the impact of Brexit on the peace process.[16] Many Northern Ireland interests also engaged with the all-island civic dialogue, delivered evidence to parliamentary inquiries (in the Houses of the Oireachtas and Westminster) and organized and participated in stakeholder events. This mobilization of civil society offered an additional site for the generation and exploration of ideas and proposals.

Taken together, these four observations identify points of commonality for a discussion about the achievement of a "flexible and imaginative" solution that is coherent and acceptable to all. In other words, there is some, albeit very limited, basis for progress in that there is broad agreement about the best outcome of the Brexit negotiations for Northern Ireland. The process issue, however, remains problematic and this is the biggest stumbling block in the search for a broad consensus as to how the softest possible Brexit might be achieved.

---

of British Industry (CBI), manufacturing trade group the EEF, the Federation of Small Businesses (FSB) and the Institute of Directors (IoD), called for the government to maintain access to the single market and customs union until a Brexit deal is reached and to prioritize the rights of EU citizens in the UK. All of these business organizations have Northern Ireland branches. One of the three economic principles for the UK's transition out of the EU outlined in the letter is: "Maintain an open frictionless border between Ireland and Northern Ireland; and between Great Britain and the island of Ireland" (letter available at: http://www.british-chambers.org.uk/press-office/press-releases/redefining-the-uks-relationship-with-the-eu-principles-for-economic-success-and-prosperity.html, accessed 2 February 2018).

15. The UFU (2017), for example, has produced a discussion document outlining its preferences and proposing options for a new domestic agricultural policy.

16. For example, the Northern Ireland Council for Voluntary Action (NICVA), the National Council for Voluntary Organizations (NCVO), the Scottish Council for Voluntary Organizations (SCVO), the Wales Council for Voluntary Action (WCVA) and The Wheel (Ireland) collectively represent over 15,200 members of voluntary and community organizations. In a joint position paper, the umbrella organizations set out a number of common principles and specific policy priorities that they believe need to be taken fully into account in the Brexit negotiations (see http://www.nicva.org/article/uk-and-irish-voluntary-and-community-sector-position-statement-on-brexit-negotiations, accessed 2 February 2018).

The dynamics of choice and compromise

The politicization of Brexit in Northern Ireland is limiting the possibilities for arriving at a consensus that accommodates (at least partially) the interests of two opposing blocs. An agreed Brexit position, however, is the preferred basis for dealing with the dilemma facing Northern Ireland. With reference to another negotiation period, that which produced the 1998 Belfast Agreement, an official of the NIO remarked: "the British government cared only that the parties agreed; for the most part, it did not care what they agreed to" (Horowitz 2002: 200). The same logic applies to Brexit. Should the Northern Ireland political parties be able to agree the terms of a special or unique or bespoke status (or any other form of settlement), it would be exceptionally difficult for the UK and Irish governments, and the EU, to resist such a proposal. Furthermore, buy-in by all parties strengthens the legitimacy of any agreed position and ensures that the prospects of implementation are high. Where parties have a stake in an agreement, it is in their interests to see that position implemented.

This is not the first time that Northern Ireland has faced seemingly insurmountable challenges in agreeing on constitutional questions. Multi-party talks have long been instrumental in shaping Northern Ireland's political future. Significantly however, a key site for multi-party discussion of Brexit was not available while the Northern Ireland Assembly and Executive were suspended. In addition to limiting the opportunities for cross-party discussion, the suspension of devolved institutions removed a vital stabilizing force in Northern Ireland politics. The absence of power-sharing institutions is symptomatic of a loss of trust between Northern Ireland's political parties. The fact of suspension engenders continuing animosity and it removes any local democratic structure for discussion of Brexit in Northern Ireland.

In his study of the choreography of the Northern Ireland peace process, Dixon (2002) suggests that former enemies had a common strategic interest in helping each other. He cites examples of the British government privately acknowledging an interest in helping Sinn Féin leader, Gerry Adams. He also notes that: "'Concessions' or restraint by republicans could help unionist leaders deliver their supporters and, vice versa, unionists could come to the aid of republicans" (Dixon 2002: 730). Often the parties "fudged" an issue, but in such a way that "each side knows that it is a 'fudge' but can live with it, and 'sell' it to their own constituents as victory, or at least not a defeat" (Bell & Cavaunagh 1998: 1356). In Northern Ireland, this approach has been used in the past to manoeuvre agreed outcomes.[17] The technique, however, has not been wholly successful. The achievement of conflict management/ resolution in Northern Ireland remains incomplete. The final phase of the peace process – the consolidation of devolved institutions and the reconciliation of communities – is proving to be its most challenging phase and Brexit is further complicating the political atmosphere. Amidst the complexity and toxicity of the current political situation, however, there may still be some prospect of finding an agreement on Northern Ireland's future after Brexit.

Pragmatism

The DUP confidence-and-supply agreement with the Conservative Party following the June 2017 general election muddied Northern Ireland's Brexit situation. DUP support for the Tories came at a financial cost to the UK exchequer. The extent to which the party also extracted political guarantees in relation to Brexit is unclear. As Anderson (2017: 13) notes however: "There is nothing in the DUP's stated agreement with Mrs. May about its attitude to the CU [Customs Union], but the border issue was almost certainly discussed and may feature in an unstated side-deal or tacit 'understanding'".

The existence or content of any such understanding is unknown. What is known, however, is that the broad unionist family has a capacity for pragmatism. It was a hallmark of their engagement with the EU during periods of devolved power (see Murphy 2014; for a commentary on the UUP see Murphy 2009). Economic pragmatism in particular, has been effective in altering behaviours and mind-sets. EU Peace funding to Northern Ireland helped to coax unionists and

---

17. Some criticize the technique and "question the morality of the price of truth exacted by the search for peace and note the toll taken by tactics such as constructive ambiguity on that crucial post-Agreement commodity – trust" (Mitchell 2009: 322). The key danger in relation to the use of constructive ambiguity in particular is that it may, ultimately and long-term, create more problems than it solves.

nationalists to create cross-community District Partnerships, where they discussed and agreed financial allocations within their local communities. In the context of Brexit, however, unionist concerns about the economic impact of Brexit co-exist with deeper concerns about its constitutional impact. For this reason, the promise of financial assistance may help to edge the political blocs towards an agreed common position.

Financial support

In Northern Ireland, during periods of instability and crisis, the promise of financial support has played a role in helping to leverage political positions. Most (if not all) political compromises in Northern Ireland have been accompanied by a financial package. Agreement on a substantial financial sum was the key price to ensure DUP support for the minority Conservative Party government following the 2017 Westminster election. The 2014 Stormont House Agreement included a comprehensive financial package worth £2 billion. It served as an important carrot in persuading Northern Ireland parties to address identity issues, introduce welfare reforms and move to make government finance more sustainable.

A financial pledge can ease the difficulties faced by negotiators in coaxing their communities to support challenging and contentious proposals. Nationalists have also called for access to EU funding in the context of their support for special status. Fianna Fáil TD and Brexit Spokesperson, Stephen Donnelly, was assured by EU Brexit negotiator Michel Barnier that the EU is willing to have a conversation about Northern Ireland access to structural funding, CAP support, Horizon 2020 and the Erasmus+ programme after the UK leaves the EU (Rothwell 2017). Such an offer is likely to emerge towards the latter end of the EU negotiation period, and it may prove to be a powerful lever in edging political parties towards reaching an agreed settlement.

Timing

In Dixon's choreographic study of the Northern Ireland peace process, he notes that timing is important in terms of helping to encourage dialogue, and ultimately agreement. The sequencing of negotiations can be vital to establishing a degree of trust between parties. Forcing discussion too early may prove counterproductive. Allowing parties and communities to adapt to a new reality and to reposition themselves may require an incremental approach rather than a giant political leap. Timing developments in such a way that parties can prepare their constituencies for what might be challenging proposals is a necessary component in successful negotiations. Deadlines are similarly important. Northern Ireland tends to treat deadlines with a degree of abandon, but where there are repercussions in terms of missing deadlines, political agreement can result. The Brexit negotiations are replete with deadlines, but it is likely that the most urgent and pressing will be close to the end of the negotiation period when a final EU–UK trading deal is being agreed. It is highly conceivable that Northern Ireland's Brexit future will remain uncertain until that deadline is reached (or breached). The future UK–EU trade relationship will indicate whether or not the UK exit from the EU is hard or soft. If the final UK–EU settlement is to result in a soft Brexit that keeps the UK within the customs union and SEM, the necessity for a bespoke Northern Ireland arrangement is undermined because there would be no need to impose a hard border on the island of Ireland. This outcome would reflect the preference of the Irish government and it would respond to unionist and nationalist support for no border on the island of Ireland. If the final UK–EU settlement, however, places the UK outside the customs union and SEM, there may be scope for unionism to consider a Brexit settlement that caters to Northern Ireland's "unique circumstances". A maximalist unionist rhetoric makes sense when there is no clarity about the final UK Brexit deal. Indeed there may even be a change of UK leadership before Brexit negotiations are completed, resulting in altered UK Brexit preferences. Unionists are not willing to pre-emptively differentiate Northern Ireland from the rest of the UK. Agreeing a potentially unnecessary outcome at the outset of the negotiation period (i.e. some form of special status) is manifestly not in the longer-term interests of unionism. For unionists, the timing of Northern Ireland Brexit developments is likely to follow rather than pre-empt wider UK–EU negotiations. Intransigence may yield to engagement, but political patience is likely to be tested along the way.

Language

The language and symbolism used by leaders and parties to frame political discussions around Brexit is hugely important. The various contested meanings that attach to specific words, terms and narratives are not to be underestimated for they have an ability to derail well-intentioned political proposals. There is some evidence of sensitivity to language *vis-à-vis* Brexit discussions in Northern Ireland. The Irish government, for example, shied away from references to "special status" for Northern Ireland because of its specific connotations for unionists. However, the language, tone and approach articulated by Taoiseach Leo Varadkar troubled unionists. Gudgin (2017) noted:

> Until last June [2017] the Irish Prime Minister, Enda Kenny, had fully cooperated with the authorities in Northern Ireland. Quiet meetings on Brexit took place between civil servants in Ireland and Northern Ireland. Constructive work took place in preparation for an electronic border. When the new Taoiseach, Leo Varadkar took over in June all of this stopped and a harder line emerged from Dublin.

Brexit has led to increased unionist distrust of Dublin and prompted strong suspicions that the Irish government is intent on using Brexit to progress an Irish unity agenda. Unionist faith in the British government, as the defender of unionist principles, however, is also tenuous. Prime Minister Theresa May's plans to agree proposals for the Irish border with the EU without full DUP approval was greeted with alarm by the broad unionist family. The language of the proposal was insensitive to unionism. UUP leader, Robin Swann (2017), stated: "whoever thought the proposals were acceptable to the unionist population of Northern Ireland and throughout the United Kingdom, clearly had no understanding of unionists or unionism".

Northern Ireland unionists occupy a dubious place where they are wary of the Republic of Ireland, and feel vulnerable to a British government that often misunderstands them. This feeds unionist insecurity and promotes a spirit of defensiveness that is highly sensitized to language and tone. In this context, the avoidance of ambiguous or loaded language is imperative. Former Northern Ireland Secretary of

State James Brokenshire's language suggests some sensitivity to union-ism (Ferguson 2017, emphasis added): "As Secretary of State I am fully committed to ensuring that, as negotiations progress, the interests of Northern Ireland are protected and advanced, through the develop-ment of *specific solutions* to address its *unique circumstances*".

The use of measured language can be effective, but there is also a need to avoid the use of antagonistic language. Talk of a border poll was met with derision by unionists when Sinn Féin first voiced support for it in the days after the EU referendum. The Sinn Féin move was futile in that there was insufficient support for a border poll. However, by placing such a polarizing issue on the political agenda, Sinn Féin riled unionists, forcing them into a defensive position and alienating them at an early point in the Brexit process.

Different interpretations can also be used to depict proposals as a win-win opportunity for all parties. This requires attaching specific meanings to proposals and persuading parties that these meet their core interests, that is creating a scenario where neither side is seen to either win or lose, and where key unionist and nationalist principles can be maintained according to their own interpretation. Farrington (2006: 291) notes that in Northern Ireland: "Interpretations of the political environment are immediate political issues affecting the outcomes of initiatives". Factoring in partisan and communal understandings of specific proposals, being sensitive to the language in which proposals are presented and appreciating that constraining contextual factors exist, is important to creating a constructive and unthreatening nego-tiating environment.

Dynamics

There are a range of contextual factors that impact on the troubled and tense political environment in Northern Ireland, characterized here as a "negative peace". This type of environment breeds mistrust and sus-picion. It means that parties are wary of the intentions and motives of their political opponents. An unhealthy amount of scepticism such as this, can constrain the ability of parties to engage and may pro-duce insurmountable obstacles to the achievement of agreement. In Northern Ireland, there are various factors that undermine the integrity of the negotiating environment.

The political rise of Sinn Féin has been a recent feature of politics north and south of the border, and the electoral growth of the party has become particularly evident since the early 2000s. Sinn Féin has effectively morphed into a mainstream political party without abandoning its core constitutional aspirations. The death of Sinn Féin's Martin McGuinness in 2017, and the decision by Sinn Féin President Gerry Adams to step down as party leader in 2018 (after 35 years at the helm), marked a generational shift in the party that may further broaden its future electoral appeal. To date, the party's electoral growth has allowed it to play a leadership role in Northern Ireland through its membership of the Executive. Sinn Féin is a smaller political force in the Republic of Ireland, but there is some likelihood that the party may emerge as the kingmaker in future elections in the Republic of Ireland. All of the main Irish political parties – Fine Gael, Fianna Fáil and the Labour Party – claim that they would not enter a coalition with Sinn Féin, but until such a scenario arrives, it is difficult to test their resolve. Electoral signs in Northern Ireland also point to a party on the up. The prospect of Sinn Féin emerging as the largest political party in Northern Ireland in the near future is a realistic one. Brexit potentially elevates this likelihood because Brexit plays into Sinn Féin's broader republican narrative by creating an enhanced logic for the pursuit of a united Ireland. Should Brexit prove to be economically damaging to Northern Ireland, calls for a united Ireland are likely to grow. There are suspicions, however, that Sinn Féin's support for special status may in fact mask a preference for a hard border. Such a border would be more economically damaging for Northern Ireland, and thus more likely to produce support for a border poll. Unionist suspicions that Sinn Féin may be manipulating Brexit to engineer increased support for such an outcome contributes to a negative and deeply dysfunctional political environment.

The Irish government is also an important player in the Brexit process. A steadfast determination to avoid a hard border on the island of Ireland, and a doggedness about not contributing to the design of any such border, antagonized unionists who objected to the harsher tone adopted by the Irish government. Unionism perceived the Irish failure to engage more robustly with the border issue as an indication of their nationalist sympathies. There is some sense of betrayal felt by unionism in relation to the Irish government's motives, which appear to side decisively with one community over another (although the same might be said for the British government's unionist sympathies). There is also an awareness that the Republic of Ireland has a stake in the EU negotiations, and will have some leverage in terms of pushing for a settlement at the EU level that meets Irish national interests. Exercising the veto may not be something the Irish government contemplates (although Sinn Féin has called for them to do so if necessary). The unionist interpretation of Irish government intentions means that they harbour serious concerns about how their interests may be marginalized by an Irish government intent on prioritizing its own narrow interests.

Unionism, however, does possess some critical safeguards. DUP support for the minority Conservative Party government offers the party its own leverage in terms of protecting unionist concerns. The EU negotiators have made it clear that they will consider any proposals *from the UK government* that deal with the Northern Ireland question. The ball is firmly in the UK government's court and the DUP has their ear. Such is the slimness of the Conservative Party's hold on power that their dependence on DUP support is heavy and was vividly illustrated when the Prime Minister Theresa May pulled out of an agreement with the EU negotiating team in December 2017 following a phone call from DUP leader Arlene Foster. From a nationalist interpretation, this points to a British government that is biased towards a UK–EU (and Northern Ireland) settlement that favours unionist interests and aspirations. Vocal nationalist support for special status is premised on the belief that nationalists cannot be guaranteed a fair hearing from the UK government such is the depth of their reliance on the DUP.

Necessity

There is an urgency and seriousness to the Brexit issue for Northern Ireland. It represents the most profound challenge to Northern Ireland's future and could have a severe destabilizing impact on the whole island. Brexit, therefore, is ostensibly about Northern Ireland's economic and political well-being, and potentially about possible future constitutional developments. Lessons from earlier periods of negotiation suggest that there is a need for forward thinking in terms of possible future political and constitutional developments and an attendant need for parties to future-proof their preferences and aspirations. By not engaging in a dialogue, the parties in Northern Ireland risk being completely ostracized from the broader debates and dialogues that are ongoing in London and Brussels. With or without Northern Ireland input, the UK is set to leave the EU. An imposed settlement – which is not informed or influenced by direct input from Northern Ireland political parties – is undesirable for both communities. It may not command the necessary legitimacy for it to be broadly acceptable, and opposition to its terms may propel Northern Ireland backwards. The EU referendum reopened old constitutional quarrels in Northern Ireland and it has complicated the process of ending those quarrels once and for all. In effect, Brexit is the biggest test to face Northern Ireland since the signing of the 1998 Belfast Agreement. If Brexit is to be effectively navigated and if Northern Ireland's future is to be safeguarded, there is a necessity for unionists and nationalists to confront hugely difficult and challenging choices. The very future of the polity may depend on such efforts.

Conclusion

It is clear that Brexit presents Northern Ireland with very considerable economic and political challenges. Neutralizing the worst impact is best met by political opponents in Northern Ireland forging agreement on the shape of Northern Ireland's future relationship with the EU, as part of the UK. The long-term absence of a Northern Ireland Executive (since January 2017) paralysed any ability to forge a position on Northern Ireland's future outside the EU. Internal legacy issues, shifting electoral dynamics, strategic party positioning, a political environment that breeds suspicion and mistrust, and opposing perspectives on Brexit impinged on the ability of key political actors in Northern Ireland to respond collectively to an altered political reality. Northern Ireland's "negative peace" served as an obstacle to dealing with complex and politicized Brexit-related challenges and prevented agreement on what is possible and desirable in planning for a future outside the EU. The danger, however, is that without agreement, Brexit may ultimately unleash dynamics that have the potential for profound and troubling consequences not just for Northern Ireland, but for the UK as a whole, for the Republic of Ireland and for the EU.

The fate of Northern Ireland is dependent on the words and actions of others. Nationalists and the Irish government support special arrangements for Northern Ireland. The British government and unionists strongly object to such a formula. There is no evident or obvious compromise acceptable to both unionists and nationalists. This speaks to the acute political sensitivities that Brexit has evoked in Northern Ireland and it points to the extraordinary dilemmas facing Britain in its attempts to deal with the Northern Ireland-Brexit quandary. Dependent on the DUP, the UK government is highly sensitive to unionist objections to special status, and also keen to protect the territorial integrity of the United Kingdom. Yet there are no alternative proposals that offer comparable protection for Northern Ireland interests. The UK government faces hard and unpalatable choices in dealing with its Brexit outlier. A failure to contemplate those choices and/or a failure to find agreement within Northern Ireland risks undermining the very thing that the British government and unionism seek to protect, namely the unity of the UK. A hard border and a possible economic downturn may well produce serious instability, and lead to irresistible pressures for constitutional change on the island of Ireland. Special status offers a means to thwart and quieten those forces, to ensure political and economic stability and to maintain the constitutional status quo in Northern Ireland.

Today, Europe and Northern Ireland's future are inextricably linked in utterly unexpected ways. Negotiating a special EU deal for Northern Ireland may be hugely challenging and contentious, but it may also prove to be the most effective route to staving off more widespread political and constitutional instability.

References

"A new kind of trouble", *The Economist*, 22 January 2015.

"A step into the unknown", *Belfast Telegraph*, 25 June 2016.

"'A tremendous wrench': Sir Ivan Rogers' resignation email in full", *The Guardian*, 4 January 2017, available at: https://www.theguardian.com/politics/2017/jan/04/quote-sir-ivan-rogers-resignation-eu-brexit-email-in-full.

"Agreement between the Conservative and Unionist Party and the Democratic Unionist Party on support for the government in parliament", 26 June 2017, available at: https://www.gov.uk/government/uploads/system/uploads/attachment_data/file/621794/Confidence_and_Supply_Agreement_between_the_Conservative_Party_and_the_DUP.pdf.

"An Irish passport does not make you less unionist: MP", *The News Letter*, 29 June 2016, available at: https://www.newsletter.co.uk/news/an-irish-passport-does-not-make-you-less-unionist-mp-1-7453914.

Anderson, J. (2017) "A solution to the problem of a 'hard' Irish border: The island's post-Brexit borders", Invited submission to the Seanad Éireann (Irish Senate) Special Select Parliamentary on the Withdrawal of the United Kingdom from the European Union, 12 June, available at: http://crossborder.ie/site2015/wp-content/uploads/2017/07/REVISED-Solution-Irish-Border-Problem-pdf-2-July-.pdf.

Armstrong, K. (2017) *Brexit Time: Leaving the EU – How, Why and When?* Cambridge: Cambridge University Press.

Azrout, R. & C. de Vreese (2017) "The moderating role of identification and campaign exposure in party cueing effects", *West European Politics*, early view, 4 October.

Barnier, M. (2017) "Address to both Houses of the Oireachtas", Leinster House, Dublin, 11 May, available at: https://ec.europa.eu/ireland/news/eu-chief-negotiator-michel-barnier-addresses-both-houses-of-the-oireachtas_en.

Barrett, A. *et al.* (2015) "Scoping the possible economic implications of Brexit on Ireland", ERSI Research Series No. 48, November.

BBC News (2016) "Boris Johnson: Brexit would not affect Irish border", 29 February, available at: http://www.bbc.com/news/uk-northern-ireland-35692452.

Bell, C. & K. Cavaunagh (1998) "Constructive ambiguity or internal self-determination? Self-determination, group accommodation, and the Belfast Agreement", *Fordham International Law Journal* 22 (4): 1345–71.

Birnie, E. & G. Brownlow (2017) "Should the fiscal powers of the Northern Ireland Assembly be enhanced?", *Regional Studies* 51 (9): 1429–39.

Birrell, D. & D. Heenan (2017) "The continuing volatility of devolution in Northern Ireland: The shadow of direct rule", *Political Quarterly* 88 (3): 473–9.

Boffey, D. (2017) "Brexit: UK likely to end up with Canadian-style deal, warns Barnier", The Guardian, 24 October, available at: https://www.the-guardian.com/politics/2017/oct/23/uk-likely-to-end-up-with-canadian-style-deal-warns-michel-barnier.

Booth, S. *et al.* (2015) "What if...? The consequences, challenges and opportunities facing Britain outside EU", Open Europe Report 03, available at: http://2ihmoy1d3v7630ar9h2rsglp-wpengine.netdna-ssl.com/wp-content/uploads/2015/03/150507-Open-Europe-What-If-Report-Final-Digital-Copy.pdf.

Breinlich, H. *et al.* (2017) "The Brexit vote, inflation and UK living standards", Paper 111, Centre for Economic Performance, LSE, available at: http://cep.lse.ac.uk/pubs/download/brexit11.pdf.

"Brexit no threat to Northern Ireland, claims Nigel Farage", *Irish Times*, 2 March 2016, available at: http://www.irishtimes.com/news/ireland/irish-news/brexit-no-threat-to-northern-ireland-claims-nigel-farage-1.2556145.

Bristow, S. (1975) "Partisanship, participation and legitimacy in Britain's EEC referendum", *Journal of Common Market Studies* 14 (4): 297–310.

Brownlow, G. (2017) "Practice running ahead of theory? Political economy and the economic lessons of UK devolution", *Cambridge Journal of Regions, Economy and Society* 10 (3): 559–73.

Buchanan, S. (2008) "Transforming conflict in Northern Ireland and the border counties: Some lessons from the Peace Programmes on valuing participative democracy", *Irish Political Studies* 23 (3): 387–409.

Budd, L. (2015) "The consequences for the Northern Ireland economy from a United Kingdom exit from the European Union", Briefing Note: CETI/OU, 2/15, March.

Budd, L. (2017) "Stalling or breaking? Northern Ireland's economy in the balance", in D. Bailey & L. Budd (eds), *The Political Economy of Brexit*, 111–28. Newcastle upon Tyne: Agenda Publishing.

Bullman, U. (1997) "The politics of the third level", in C. Jeffrey (ed.), *The Regional Dimension of the EU: Towards a Third Level in Europe?*, 3–19. London: Frank Cass.

Campbell, K., D. Wilson & J. Braithwaite (2016) "Ending residual paramilitary domination in Northern Ireland? Restorative economic and social inclusion strategies", Working Paper in association with the Understanding Conflict Trust (Northern Ireland), available at: http://uir.ulster.ac.uk/36409/1/campbell%2C%20wilson%20%26%20Braithwaite%20NI%20Regnet%20working%20paper%20.pdf.

Carmichael, P. (2016) "Reflections from Northern Ireland on the result of the UK referendum on EU membership", in M. Guderjan (ed.), *The Future of the UK: Between Internal and External Divisions*, 82–101. Berlin: Humboldt University.

Centre for Cross Border Studies (2016) "The UK referendum on membership of the EU: Citizen mobility", EU Referendum Briefing Paper No. 4, 20 June, available at: http://crossborder.ie/site2015/wp-content/uploads/2016/06/CCBS-and-Cooperation-Ireland-EU-Referendum-Briefing-Paper-4.pdf.

Clarke, H., M. Goodwin & P. Whiteley (2017) "Why Britain voted for Brexit: An individual-level analysis of the 2016 referendum vote", *Parliamentary Affairs* 70 (3): 439–64.

Coakley, J. & J. Garry (2016) "Northern Ireland: The challenge of public opinion", *QPol*, 9 December, available at: http://qpol.qub.ac.uk/public-opinion-challenge-ni/.

Collins, S. (2017) "Kenny has delivered on first round of Brexit talks", *Irish Times*, 27 April, available at: http://www.irishtimes.com/opinion/stephen-collins-kenny-has-delivered-on-first-round-of-brexit-talks-1.3062157.

Connolly, T. (2017a) *Brexit and Ireland: The Dangers, the Opportunities, and the Inside Story of the Irish Response*. Dublin: Penguin Ireland.

Connolly, T. (2017b) "The Brexit veto: How and why Ireland raised the stakes", *RTE News*, 19 November, available at: https://www.rte.ie/news/analysis-and-comment/2017/1117/920981-long-read-brexit/.

Coulter, C. (2014) "Under which constitutional arrangement would you still prefer to be unemployed? Neoliberalism, the peace process, and the politics of class in Northern Ireland", *Studies in Conflict and Terrorism* 37 (9): 763–76.

Coveney, S. (2017) "Technology alone can never solve a political quandary like Brexit", *Belfast Telegraph*, 17 August, available at: http://www.belfast-telegraph.co.uk/opinion/news-analysis/simon-coveney-technology-alone-can-never-solve-a-political-quandary-like-brexit-36039593.html.

Curtice, J. (2017) "Why Leave won the UK's EU referendum", *Journal of Common Market Studies Annual Review* 55: 19–37.

Danske Bank (2017) "Northern Ireland quarterly sectoral forecasts (Q2)", available at: http://www.danskebank.co.uk/SiteCollectionDocuments/economic/2017/Danske-Bank-Northern-Ireland-Quarterly-Sectoral-Forecasts-2017-Q2.pdf.

Davis, D. (2016) Speech on Brexit delivered at the Institute of Chartered Engineers, London, 4 February, available at: http://www.daviddavismp.com/david-davis-speech-on-brexit-at-the-institute-of-chartered-engineers/.

De Wilde, P., A. Leupold & H. Schmidtke (2016) "Introduction: The differentiated politicisation of European governance", *West European Politics* 39 (1): 3–22.

Department of the Taoiseach (2014) *National Risk Assessment 2014*, Dublin: Department of the Taoiseach, available at: https://www.taoiseach.gov.ie/eng/Publications/Publications_2014/National_Risk_Assessment_report_2014.pdf.

Department of the Taoiseach (2016) *National Risk Assessment 2016*, Dublin: Department of the Taoiseach, available at: https://www.taoiseach.gov.ie/eng/Publications/Publications_2016/2016_National_Risk_Assessment.pdf.

Dhingra, S. *et al.* (2016) "The UK Treasury analysis of 'The long-term economic impact of EU membership and the alternatives'", CEP Commentary, Paper Brexit 04, available at: http://cep.lse.ac.uk/pubs/download/brexit04.pdf.

Dixon, P. (2002) "Political skills or lying and manipulation? The choreography of the Northern Ireland peace process", *Political Studies* 50 (4): 725–41.

Doherty, B. *et al.* (2017) "Northern Ireland and Brexit: The European Economic Area option", EPC Discussion Paper, 7 April, available at: http://epc.eu/documents/uploads/pub_7576_northernirelandandbrexit.pdf.

Doyle, K. (2017) "We won't help the UK come up with border solution – Leo Varadkar", *Irish Independent*, 28 July, available at: https://www.independent.ie/business/brexit/we-wont-help-the-uk-come-up-with-border-solution-leo-varadkar-35977592.html.

Duggan, J. (2017) "Q&A: Ireland's Leo Varadkar on Brexit, Trump and keeping Ireland 'at the center of the world'", *Time Magazine*, 13 July.

DUP (2016a) "Foster – 'We will on balance recommend a vote to leave the EU'", *Press release*, 20 February, available at: http://www.mydup.com/news/article/foster-we-will-on-balance-recommend-a-vote-to-leave-the.eu.

DUP (2016b) "Dodds – 'Enda Kenny should respect role of UK voters'", *Press release*, 25 January, available at: http://www.mydup.com/news/article/dodds-enda-kenny-should-respect-role-of-uk-voters.

DUP (2017) "Our plan for Northern Ireland: The DUP manifesto for the 2017 Northern Ireland Assembly election", Belfast: DUP, available at: http://www.mydup.com/images/uploads/publications/DUP_Manifesto_2017_v2_SINGLES.pdf.

"DUP leader Arlene Foster wants to bring stability to UK with Conservatives", *The Guardian*, 9 June 2017, available at: https://www.theguardian.com/politics/2017/jun/09/theresa-may-reaches-deal-with-dup-to-form-government-after-shock-election-result-northern-Ireland.

Ecker-Ehrhardt, M. & M. Zürn (2013) "Die Politisierung der Weltpolitik" [The Politicization of World Politics], in M. Zürn & M. Ecker-Ehrhardt (eds), *Die Politisierung der Weltpolitik: Umkämpfte internationale Institutionen* [*The Politicization of World Politics: Contested International Institutions*], 335–67. Berlin: Suhrkamp.

"EU's border stance paves way for Northern Ireland to get special status", *The Guardian*, 1 September 2017, available at: https://www.theguardian. com/politics/2017/sep/01/eu-irish-border-stance-paves-way-northern-ireland-special-status-brexit.

European Commission (2007) "Attitudes towards the EU in the United Kingdom", Flash Eurobarometer No. 203, May, available at: http:// ec.europa.eu/commfrontoffice/publicopinion/flash/fl203_en.pdf.

European Commission (2017) "Communication from the European Commission to the European Council (Art 50) on the state of progress of the negotiations with the United Kingdom under Article 50 of the Treaty on European Union", COM(2017) 784 final, 8 December, Brussels, available at: https://ec.europa. eu/commission/sites/beta-political/files/1_en_act_communication.pdf.

European Council (2017) "Guidelines following the United Kingdom's notification under Article 50", EUCO XT 20004/17, 29 April, available at: http:// www.consilium.europa.eu/en/press/press-releases/2017/04/29-euco-brexit-guidelines/.

European Parliament (Directorate General for Internal Affairs) (2017) "An assessment of the economic impact of Brexit on the EU27: Study for the IMCO Committee", IP/A/IMCO/2016-13, March, available at: http://www.europarl.europa.eu/RegData/etudes/STUD/2017/595374/ IPOL_STU(2017)595374_EN.pdf.

EY (2017) "Could uncertainty be your best opportunity? Economic Eye summer forecast 2017", available at: http://www.ey.com/Publication/ vwLUAssets/ey-economic-eye-Marketing-Brochure-2017/$File/ey-economic-eye-Marketing-Brochure-2017.pdf.

Farrington, C. (2006) "Unionism and the peace process in Northern Ireland", *British Journal of Politics and International Relations* 8 (2): 277–94.

Farry, S. (2009) "Consociationalism and the creation of a shared future for Northern Ireland", in R. Taylor (ed.), *Consociational Theory: McGarry and O'Leary and the Northern Ireland Conflict*, 164–79. London: Routledge.

Farry, S. (2017) "Assembly missing chance to have any say on 'Great Repeal Bill'", *Irish News*, 5 September, available at: http://www.irishnews.com/ news/2017/09/05/news/assembly-missing-chance-to-have-say-on-great-repeal-bill--1127883/.

Ferguson, A. (2017) "Brokenshire to discuss impact of Brexit on NI with EU figures", *Irish Times*, 6 November, available at: https://www.irishtimes.

com/news/ireland/irish-news/brokenshire-to-discuss-impact-of-brexit-on-ni-with-eu-figures-1.3281056.

Flanagan, C. (2015) "What Brexit means for Northern Ireland", Speech by Minister for Foreign Affairs and Trade, Mr Charlie Flanagan TD, Queen's University Belfast, 26 November, available at: https://www.dfa.ie/news-and-media/speeches/speeches-archive/2015/november/what-brexit-means-for-northern-ireland/.

"Former PSNI Chief Constable Hugh Orde scaremongering over risks to border of a Brexit, rages DUP MP Sammy Wilson", *Belfast Telegraph*, 1 June, available at: http://www.belfasttelegraph.co.uk/news/northern-ireland/former-psni-chief-constable-hugh-orde-scaremongering-over-risks-to-border-of-a-brexit-rages-dup-mp-sammy-wilson-34762491.html.

Galtung, J. (1964) "An editorial", *Journal of Peace Research* 1 (1): 2.

Galtung, J. (1990) "Cultural violence", *Journal of Peace Research* 27 (3): 291–305.

Ganiel, G. (2009) "'Battling in Brussels': The DUP and the European Union", *Irish Political Studies* 24 (4): 575–88.

Garry, J. (2016) "The EU referendum vote in Northern Ireland: Implications for our understanding of citizens' political views and behaviour", Northern Ireland Assembly Knowledge Exchange Seminar Series 2016–2017, available at: http://www.niassembly.gov.uk/globalassets/documents/raise/knowledge_exchange/briefing_papers/series6/garry121016.pdf.

George, S. (1998) *An Awkward Partner: Britain in the European Community* (3rd edition), Oxford: Oxford University Press.

Gilmore, A. (2017) "Hard borders of the mind: Brexit, Northern Ireland and the Good Friday Agreement", ECFR Commentary, 13 April, available at: http://www.ecfr.eu/article/commentary_hard_borders_of_the_mind_brexit_northern_ireland_and_the_7273.

Glencross, A. (2016) *Why the UK Voted for Brexit: David Cameron's Great Miscalculation*, Basingstoke: Palgrave.

Goodwin, M. & O. Heath (2016) "The 2016 referendum, Brexit and the left behind: An aggregate level analysis of the result", *Political Quarterly* 87 (3): 323–32.

Gordon, M. (2016) "The UK's sovereignty situation: Brexit, bewilderment and beyond …", *King's Law Journal* 27 (3): 333–43.

Gormley-Heenan, C. & A. Aughey (2017) "Northern Ireland and Brexit: Three effects on 'the border in the mind'", *British Journal of Politics and International Relations* 19 (3): 497–511.

Gormley-Heenan, C., A. Aughey & P. Devine (2017) "Waking up in a different country: Brexit and Northern Ireland", Ark Northern Ireland Research

Update No. 116, June, available at: http://www.ark.ac.uk/publications/ updates/update116.pdf.

Gough, A. & E. Magennis (2009) "The impact of devolution on everyday life, 1999–2009: The case of cross-border commerce", Working Papers in British-Irish Studies No. 85, Institute for British-Irish Studies, University College Dublin, available at: http://researchrepository.ucd.ie/bitstream/ handle/10197/2392/85_gough-magennis.pdf?sequence=1.

"Government says Northern Ireland needs 'special status' after Brexit", *RTE News*, 23 June, available at: https://www.rte.ie/news/brexit/2017/0622/ 884832-coveney-ireland-brexit/.

Greer, J. (2016) "After 41 years of shifting battlelines, the Brexit vote for Northern Ireland is a very tough one to call", *Belfast Telegraph*, 23 May, available at: http://www.belfasttelegraph.co.uk/opinion/news-analysis/after-41-years-of-shifting-battlelines-the-brexit-vote-for-northern-ireland-is-a-very-tough-one-to-call-34736918.html.

Gudgin, G. (2000) "Europe and the Northern Ireland economy", in D. Kennedy (ed.), *Living with the European Union: The Northern Ireland Experience*, 38–70. Basingstoke: Palgrave.

Gudgin, G. (2017) "For the DUP, the border question is raw identity politics", *The Guardian*, 7 December, available at: https://www.theguardian.com/ commentisfree/2017/dec/07/dup-border-identity-britain-irish-northern-Ireland.

Guelke, A. (1988) *Northern Ireland: The International Perspective*, Dublin: Gill & Macmillan.

Haagerup, N. (1984) "Report drawn up on behalf of the Political Affairs Committee on the situation in Northern Ireland", European Parliament Working Document, 1–1526/83, 9 March.

Hainsworth, P. (1996) "Northern Ireland and the European Union", in A. Aughey & D. Morrow (eds), *Northern Ireland Politics*, 129–38. London: Routledge.

Hayward, K. (2017a) Bordering on Brexit: Views from local communities in the central border region of Ireland/Northern Ireland, A report prepared for ICBAN, November, available at: http://www.qub.ac.uk/brexit/ Brexitfilestore/Filetoupload,781170,en.pdf.

Hayward, K. (2017b) "A Brexit border in the Irish Sea was never really on the table", *RTE Brainstorm*, 25 September, available at: https://www.rte.ie/eile/ brainstorm/2017/0801/894406-a-posbrexit-border-in-the-irish-sea-was-never-really-on-the-table/.

Hayward, K. & M. Murphy (2012) "The (soft) power of commitment: The EU and conflict resolution in Northern Ireland", *Ethnopolitics* 11 (4): 439–52.

Henderson, A. *et al.* (2017) "How Brexit was made in England", *British Journal of Politics and International Affairs*, early view.

HM Government (2016) "HM Treasury analysis: The long-term economic impact of EU membership and the alternatives", Cm 9250, April, available at: https://www.gov.uk/government/uploads/system/uploads/attachment_data/file/517415/treasury_analysis_economic_impact_of_eu_membership_web.pdf.

HM Government (2017a) "Northern Ireland and Ireland: Position paper", 16 August, available at: https://www.gov.uk/government/publications/northern-ireland-and-ireland-a-position-paper.

HM Government (2017b) "The United Kingdom's exit from and new partnership with the European Union", Cm 9417, February, available at: https://www.gov.uk/government/uploads/system/uploads/attachment_data/file/589191/The_United_Kingdoms_exit_from_and_partnership_with_the_EU_Web.pdf.

Hobolt, S. (2009) *Europe in Question: Referendums on European Integration*, Oxford: Oxford University Press.

Hobolt, S. (2016) "The Brexit vote: A divided nation, a divided continent", *Journal of European Public Policy* 3 (9): 1259–77.

Holland, C. & G. Rabrenovic (2017) "Social immobility, ethno-politics, and sectarian violence: Obstacles to post-conflict reconstruction in Northern Ireland", *International Journal of Politics, Culture and Society* 30 (3): 219–44.

Hooghe, L. & G. Marks (2005) "Calculation, community and cues: Public opinion on European integration", *European Union Politics* 6 (4): 419–43.

Hooghe, L. & G. Marks (2009) "A postfunctionalist theory of European integration: From permissive consensus to constraining dissensus", *British Journal of Politics and International Relations* 39 (1): 1–23.

Horowitz, D. (2002) "Explaining the Northern Ireland agreement: The sources of an unlikely constitutional consensus", *British Journal of Political Science* 32: 93–220.

House of Commons Foreign Affairs Committee (2016) "Equipping the government for Brexit", HC 431, 20 July, available at: https://publications.parliament.uk/pa/cm201617/cmselect/cmfaff/431/431.pdf.

House of Commons Northern Ireland Affairs Committee (2016) "Northern Ireland and the EU referendum", HC 48, 25 May, available at: https://publications.parliament.uk/pa/cm201617/cmselect/cmniaf/48/48.pdf.

House of Commons Northern Ireland Affairs Committee (2017) "Electricity sector in Northern Ireland", HC 51, 1 May, available at: https://publications.parliament.uk/pa/cm201617/cmselect/cmniaf/51/51.pdf.

House of Lords European Union Committee (2016) "Brexit: UK-Irish relations", HL Paper 76, 12 December, available at: https://publications.parliament.uk/pa/ld201617/ldselect/ldeucom/76/76.pdf.

House of Lords European Union Committee (2017) "Brexit: Devolution",

HL Paper 9, 19 July, available at: https://publications.parliament.uk/pa/ld201719/ldselect/ldeucom/9/9.pdf.

Huttl, P. & J. Romero (2016) "Northern Ireland and EU funds", Bruegel blog post, available at: http://bruegel.org/2016/05/northern-ireland-and-eu-funds/.

Irish Farmers' Association (IFA) (2017) "Brexit: The imperatives for Irish farmers and the agri-food sector", IFA Policy Paper, March, available at: https://www.ifa.ie/wp-content/uploads/2017/03/763773Brexit-imperatives-policy-paper55629.pdf.

Irish Government (2017) "Ireland and the negotiations on the UK's withdrawal from the European Union: The Government's approach", Dublin: Irish Government Publication, available at: https://merrionstreet.ie/en/EU-UK/Key_Irish_Documents/Government_Approach_to_Brexit_Negotiations.pdf.

Joint Committee on European Union Affairs (2015) "UK/EU future relationship: Implications for Ireland", June, available at: http://seankyne.ie/wp-content/uploads/2015/06/23-6-15-Report-UK-EU-Future-Relations.pdf.

Joint Committee on the Implementation of the Good Friday Agreement (2017) "Brexit and the future of Ireland: Uniting Ireland and its people in peace and prosperity", 32/JCIGFA/02, August, available at: https://data.oireachtas.ie/ie/oireachtas/committee/dail/32/joint_committee_on_the_implementation_of_the_good_friday_agreement/reports/2017/2017-08-02_brexit-and-the-future-of-ireland-uniting-ireland-and-its-people-in-peace-and-prosperity_en.pdf.

"Joint Report from the negotiators of the European Union and the United Kingdom government on progress during Phase 1 of negotiations under Article 50 TEU on the United Kingdom's orderly withdrawal from the European Union", 8 December 2017, available at: https://ec.europa.eu/commission/publications/joint-report-negotiators-european-union-and-united-kingdom-government-progress-during-phase-1-negotiations-under-article-50-teu-united-kingdoms-orderly-withdrawal-european-union_en.

Keating, M., P. Cairney & E. Hepburn (2009) "Territorial policy communities and devolution in the UK", *Cambridge Journal of Regions, Economy and Society* 2 (1): 51–66.

Keep, M. & P. Brien (2017) "Public expenditure by country and region", House of Commons Library Briefing Paper No. 04033, 30 November, available at: http://researchbriefings.parliament.uk/ResearchBriefing/Summary/SN04033#fullreport.

Kelly, F. (2016) "Brexit: Grass greener if we leave say Northern Irish farmers", *Irish Times*, 22 June, available at: https://www.irishtimes.com/news/politics/brexit-grass-greener-if-we-leave-say-northern-irish-farmers-1.2693820.

Knox, C. (2016) "Northern Ireland: Where is the peace dividend?", *Policy and Politics* 44 (3): 485–503.

Labour Party (2017) "A Labour Party perspective on Brexit", available at: https://www.labour.ie/download/pdf/a_labour_party_perspective_on_brexit.pdf.

Lederach, J. (2014) *The Little Book of Conflict Transformation*, New York: Good Books/Skyhorse Publishing.

Mac Flynn, P. (2016) "The economic implications of Brexit for Northern Ireland", NERI Working Paper Series No. 35, April, available at: https://www.nerinstitute.net/download/pdf/brexit_wp_250416.pdf.

Mac Flynn, P. (2015) "Public sector employment in Northern Ireland", NERI Research in Brief No. 20, March, available at: https://www.nerinstitute.net/download/pdf/pubsectoremploymentni.pdf.

Maillot, A. (2009) "Sinn Féin's approach to the EU: Still more 'critical' than 'engaged'?", *Irish Political Studies* 24 (4): 559–74.

Mason, R. (2016) "Boris Johnson on Brexit: 'We can be like Canada'", The Guardian, 11 March, available at: https://www.theguardian.com/politics/2016/mar/11/boris-johnson-on-brexit-we-can-be-like-canada.

Matthews, N. & J. Pow (2017) "A fresh start? The Northern Ireland Assembly election 2016", *Irish Political Studies* 32 (2): 311–26.

McAleese, D. (2017) "Calls for Brexit special status attempt to create united Ireland through back door, says UUP", *Irish News*, 1 June, available at: https://www.irishnews.com/news/generalelection/2017/06/02/news/-1042925/.

McBride, S. (2017) "MEPs cheer Jim Nicholson and reject NI special status after Brexit", *Newsletter*, 6 July, available at: http://www.newsletter.co.uk/news/meps-cheer-jim-nicholson-and-reject-ni-special-status-after-brexit-1-8042256.

McCann, G. & P. Hainsworth (2017) "Brexit and Northern Ireland: The 2016 Referendum on the United Kingdom's Membership of the European Union", *Irish Political Studies* 32 (2): 327–42.

McEwen, N. (2017) "Still better together? Purpose and power in intergovernmental councils in the UK", *Regional and Federal Studies*, early view, published online 19 October.

McGlynn, C., J. Tonge & J. McAuley (2014) "The party politics of post-devolution identity in Northern Ireland", *British Journal of Politics and International Affairs* 16 (2): 273–90.

McGowan, L. & J. O'Connor (2004) "Exploring Eurovisions: Awareness and knowledge of the European Union in Northern Ireland", *Irish Political Studies*, 19 (2): 21–42.

McGuinness, F. (2016) "Poverty in the UK: Statistics", House of Commons Library Briefing Paper No. 7096, 16 June.

"McGuinness urges vote on united Ireland in event of Brexit", *Irish Times*,

11 March 2016, available at: https://www.irishtimes.com/news/politics/mcguinness-urges-vote-on-united-ireland-in-event-of-brexit-1.2569500.

McLoughlin, P. (2009) "The SDLP and the Europeanization of the Northern Ireland problem", *Irish Political Studies* 24 (4): 603–19.

Mills, E. & C. Colvin (2016) "Why did Northern Ireland vote to Remain?", *QPol*, 18 July, available at: http://qpol.qub.ac.uk/northern-ireland-vote-remain/.

Mitchell, D. (2009) "Cooking the fudge: Constructive ambiguity and the implementation of the Northern Ireland Agreement, 1998–2007", *Irish Political Studies* 24 (3): 321–36.

Mitchell, P. (1991) "Conflict regulation and party competition in Northern Ireland", *European Journal of Political Research* 20: 67–92.

Mitchell, P. (1995) "Party competition in an ethnic dual party system", *Ethnic and Racial Studies* 18 (4): 773–96.

Mitchell, P. (1999) "The party system and party competition", in P. Mitchell & R. Wilford (eds), *Politics in Northern Ireland*, 91–116. Boulder, CO: Westview.

Moriarty, G. (2017) "Stop 'megaphone diplomacy' from Dublin over Brexit", *Irish Times*, 1 August, available at: https://www.irishtimes.com/news/ireland/irish-news/stop-megaphone-diplomacy-from-dublin-over-brexit-1.3173461.

Murphy, M. (2007) "Europeanisation and the sub-national level: Changing patterns of governance in Northern Ireland", *Regional and Federal Studies* 17 (3): 293–315.

Murphy, M. (2009) "Pragmatic politics: The Ulster Unionist Party and the European Union", *Irish Political Studies* 24 (4): 589–602.

Murphy, M. (2011) "Regional representation in Brussels and multi-level governance: Evidence from Northern Ireland", *British Journal of Politics and International Relations* 13 (4): 551–66.

Murphy, M. (2014) *Northern Ireland and the European Union: The Dynamics of a Changing Relationship*, Manchester: Manchester University Press.

Murphy, M. (2016a) "The EU referendum in Northern Ireland: Closing borders, re-opening border debates", *Journal of Contemporary European Research* 12 (4): 844–53.

Murphy, M. (2016b) "Northern Ireland and the EU referendum: The outcome, options and opportunities", *Journal of Cross Border Studies of Ireland*, 11: 18–31.

Murphy, M. (2016c) "Northern Ireland and Brexit: Now is not the time for talk of Irish unity", Blog of the Centre on Constitutional Change, 27 July, available at: http://www.centreonconstitutionalchange.ac.uk/blog/northern-ireland-and-brexit-now-not-time-talk-irish-unity.

Norris, P. (1997) "Representation and the democratic deficit", *European Journal of Political Research* 32: 273–82.

Northern Ireland Assembly (2017) "What goods does Northern Ireland export, how much are they worth and where do they go?", Research Matters Blog, 14 June, available at: http://www.assemblyresearchmatters.org/2017/06/14/goods-northern-ireland-export-much-worth-go/.

Northern Ireland Assembly Research and Information Service (2013) "European Union competitive funding in Northern Ireland", Briefing Paper, NIAR 795-13, 27 November, available at: http://www.niassembly.gov.uk/globalassets/documents/raise/publications/2013/finance_personnel/14413.pdf.

Northern Ireland Assembly Research and Information Service (2016a) "The EU referendum and potential implications for Northern Ireland", NIAR 32-16, 1 January, available at: http://www.niassembly.gov.uk/globalassets/documents/raise/publications/2016/eti/2116.pdf.

Northern Ireland Assembly Research and Information Service (2016b) "The Executive's forthcoming revised Economic Strategy for Northern Ireland: Preliminary considerations", Research and Information Service Research Paper, NIAR 414-16, 3 November, available at: http://www.niassembly.gov.uk/globalassets/documents/raise/publications/2016-2021/2016/economy/8116.pdf.

Northern Ireland Audit Office (2016) "Report by the Comptroller and Auditor General for Northern Ireland (Department of Enterprise, Trade and Investment: Resources accounts 2015–2016)", Belfast: Northern Ireland Audit Office.

Northern Ireland Executive (2012) "Economic strategy: Priorities for sustainable growth and prosperity", Belfast: Northern Ireland Executive, available at: https://www.northernireland.gov.uk/sites/default/files/publications/nigov/ni-economic-strategy-revised-130312_0.pdf.

Northern Ireland Executive (2014) "Executive's international relations strategy", February, available at: https://www.executiveoffice-ni.gov.uk/sites/default/files/publications/ofmdfm_dev/international-relations-strategy-2014.pdf.

Northern Ireland Executive (2015) "Investment strategy for Northern Ireland 2011–2021" (updated version), Belfast: Northern Ireland Executive, available at: https://www.infrastructure-ni.gov.uk/sites/default/files/publications/drd/investment-strategy-for-northern-ireland-2011-2021.pdf.

Northern Ireland Executive (2016) "Draft programme for government framework 2016–2021", Belfast: Northern Ireland Executive, available at: https://www.northernireland.gov.uk/sites/default/files/consultations/newnigov/draft-pfg-framework-2016-21.pdf.

"Northern Ireland left out as Scottish and Welsh leaders meet EU Brexit boss Barnier", *Belfast Telegraph*, 14 July 2017, available at: http://www.belfasttelegraph.co.uk/news/northern-ireland/northern-ireland-left-out-as-scottish-and-welsh-leaders-meet-eu-brexit-boss-barnier-35928657.html.

"Northern Ireland 'left without voice' on Brexit after missing Barnier talks", *Newsletter*, 13 July 2017, available at: http://www.newsletter.co.uk/news/ politics/northern-ireland-left-without-voice-on-brexit-after-missing-barnier-talks-1-8055468.

Northern Ireland Statistics and Research Agency (NISRA) (2017a) "Northern Ireland labour market report", November, available at: https://www. nisra.gov.uk/sites/nisra.gov.uk/files/publications/M4rf66-labour-market-report-november-2017.PDF.

Northern Ireland Statistics and Research Agency (NISRA) (2017b) "Quarterly employment survey", 14 June, available at: https://www.nisra.gov.uk/sites/ nisra.gov.uk/files/publications/QES%20Publication%20for%20uploadv3. pdf.

OECD (2016) "The economic consequences of Brexit: A taxing decision", OECD Economic Policy Paper No. 16, April, available at: http://www. oecd-ilibrary.org/docserver/download/5jm0lsvdkf6k-en.pdf?expires=1508 318957&id=id&accname=guest&checksum=159C7725E7005DC1E59467 F732FB7D8B.

Office for National Statistics (ONS) (2017) "Public sector employment UK", Statistical Bulletin, March, available at: https://www.ons.gov.uk/ employmentandlabourmarket/peopleinwork/publicsectorpersonnel/ bulletins/publicsectoremployment/mar2017.

O'hearn, D. (2008) "How has peace changed the Northern Irish political economy?", *Ethnopolitics* 7 (1): 101–18.

O'Toole, M. (2017) "Ireland an afterthought during Brexit campaign when I was Cameron advisor", *Irish Times*, 4 October, available at: https://www. irishtimes.com/opinion/ireland-an-afterthought-during-brexit-campaign-when-i-was-cameron-adviser-1.3242732.

Oxford Economics (2016) "Assessing the economic implications of Brexit: Executive summary", Oxford: Oxford Economics.

Paisley (Jnr), I. (2017) "Dublin is in denial about Brexit: Irish politicians urgently need to adopt a new Brexit strategy", *BrexitCentral*, 23 October, available at: http://brexitcentral.com/dublin-denial-brexit-irish-politicians-new-strategy/.

"Paisley, Tebbit and Trimble all savage idea of Brexit border in the sea", *Newsletter*, 29 July 2017, available at: http://www.newsletter.co.uk/news/ business/paisley-tebbit-and-trimble-all-savage-idea-of-brexit-border-in-the-sea-1-8078800.

Paun, A. (2017) "Finally a breakthrough with the devolved nations", Institute for Government Comment, 18 October, available at: https://www. instituteforgovernment.org.uk/blog/finally-brexit-breakthrough-devolved-nations.

Phinnemore, D. & K. Hayward (2017) "Brexit, Northern Ireland and territorial differentiation: An opportunity not to be missed", SCER Comment, 5 September, available at: https://www.scer.scot/database/ident-3334.

Power, J. (2017) "Passport applications from UK almost double after Brexit vote", *Irish Times*, 18 December, available at: https://www.irishtimes.com/news/social-affairs/passport-applications-from-uk-almost-double-after-brexit-vote-1.3331145.

PWC (2017) "Northern Ireland economic outlook: What comes next?", July, available at: https://www.pwc.co.uk/who-we-are/regions/northernireland/NIEO%20-%20July%202017.pdf.

Ramsbotham, O., T. Woodhouse & H. Miall (2011) *Contemporary Conflict Resolution* (3rd edition), Cambridge: Polity Press.

Ramsey, R. (2017) "Sharpest rise in activity in 2017 so far", *Ulster Economix*, 11 September, https://ulstereconomix.com/2017/09/11/sharpest-rise-in-activity-in-2017-so-far/#more-4528.

Rothwell, J. (2017) "Michel Barnier to offer EU funding for Northern Ireland to soften impact of Brexit", *The Telegraph*, 17 August, available at: http://www.telegraph.co.uk/news/2017/08/17/exclusive-michel-barnier-offer-eu-funding-northern-ireland-soften/.

Rowthorn, B. (1981) "Northern Ireland: An economy in crisis", *Cambridge Journal of Economics* 5: 1–31.

SDLP (2017) "Securing our future in Europe: Proposals for a special status for Northern Ireland within the EU", Belfast: SDLP, available at: http://newry.ie/attachments/article/4720/eustatus.pdf.

Shirlow, P. & C. Coulter (2014) "Northern Ireland: Twenty years after the ceasefires", *Studies in Conflict and Terrorism* 39 (9): 713–19.

Sinn Féin (2016) "The case for the North to achieve designated special status within the EU", Dublin and Belfast: Sinn Féin, available at: https://www.sinnfein.ie/files/2016/The_Case_For_The_North_To_Achieve_Special_Designated_Status_Within_The_EU.pdf.

Sinn Féin (2017a) "Martin McGuinness announces resignation as Deputy First Minister", *Press release*, 9 January, available at: http://www.sinnfein.ie/contents/42984.

Sinn Féin (2017b) "Sinn Féin Assembly manifesto 2017", Belfast: Sinn Féin, available at: https://www.sinnfein.ie/files/2017/MANIFESTO_ENGLISH.pdf.

Soares, A. (2016) "Living within and outside unions: The consequences of Brexit for Northern Ireland", *Journal of Contemporary European Research* 12 (4): 835–43.

Scottish Government (2016) "Scotland's place in Europe", Edinburgh: Scottish Government, available at: http://www.gov.scot/Resource/0051/00512073.pdf.

"Special status – a ruse to break up the UK", Statement by TUV Leader Jim Allister, 3 April 2017, available at: http://tuv.org.uk/special-status-a-ruse-to-break-up-the-uk/.

Springford, J. (2015) "Disunited kingdom: Why "Brexit" endangers Britain's poorer regions", CER Policy Brief, 7 April, available at: http://www.cer.eu/publications/archive/policy-brief/2015/disunited-kingdom-why-'brexit'-endangers-britain's-poorer-reg.

Stefanova, B. (2011) *The Europeanisation of Conflict Resolution: Regional Integration and Conflicts in Europe from the 1950s to Twenty-first Century*, Oxford: Oxford University Press.

Swann, R. (2017) "Northern Ireland is not a bargaining chip", *The Guardian*, 5 December, available at: https://www.theguardian.com/commentisfree/2017/dec/05/northern-ireland-bargaining-chip-unionists-eu-border.

Tannam, E. (2011) "Explaining British-Irish cooperation", *Review of International Studies* 37 (3): 1191–214.

"Taoiseach warns of Brexit threat to peace process", *Newstalk*, 11 May, audio available at: http://www.newstalk.com/Taoiseach-warns-of-Brexit-threat-to-peace-process.

Tonge, J. (2017a) "Supplying confidence or trouble? The deal between the Democratic Unionist Party and the Conservative Party", *Political Quarterly* 88 (3): 412–16.

Tonge, J. (2017b) "The impact and consequences of Brexit for Northern Ireland", European Parliament (Constitutional Affairs) Briefing, available at: http://www.europarl.europa.eu/RegData/etudes/BRIE/2017/583116/IPOL_BRI(2017)583116_EN.pdf.

Trimble, M. (1990) "The impact of the European Community", in R. Harris, J. Spencer & C. Jefferson (eds) *The Northern Ireland Economy*, 416–39. London: Longman.

UFU (2016) "UFU host major open EU referendum debate", *Press release*, 5 May, available at: https://www.ufuni.org/news/ufu-host-major-open-eu-referendum-debate.

UFU (2017) "Brexit: Options for a new domestic agricultural policy", UFU Discussion Document, available at: https://content17.green17creative.com/media/99/files/Brexit-Discussion-3.pdf.

UKIP (2016) "It's time for real change: Northern Ireland Assembly election manifesto", available at: https://d3n8a8pro7vhmx.cloudfront.net/ukipdev/pages/3485/attachments/original/1461660451/ukip2016NImanifesto.pdf?1461660451.

UUP (2014) "European manifesto 2014", Belfast: UUP, available at: https://uup.org/assets/images/european%20manifesto%20twentyfourteen.pdf.

UUP (2016a) "Statement from the Ulster Unionist Party", *Press release*, 5 March, available at: https://uup.org/news/4155/Statement-from-the-Ulster-Unionist-Party#.WdOySHj1JE4.

UUP (2016b) "A vision for Northern Ireland outside the EU", Belfast: UUP, available at: https://uup.org/assets/images/a%20vision%20for%20ni%20outside%20the%20eu.pdf.

UUP (2017a) "Special status will put us on the fringes of the Union – Kinahan", *Press release*, 6 May, available at: https://uup.org/news/4983/21/Special-status-will-put-us-on-the-fringes-of-the-Union-Kinahan#.Wf9wMXijBE4.

UUP (2017b) "Nicholson dismisses calls for NI 'special status' post-Brexit as unworkable", *Press release*, 10 February, available at: https://uup.org/news/4844/Nicholson-dismisses-calls-for-NI-special-status-post-Brexit-as-unworkable#.Wf7guHijBE4.

Varadkar, L. (2017) "The future of relationships North and South", Speech by the Taoiseach Mr Leo Varadkar TD, Queen's University Belfast, 4 August, available at: https://www.taoiseach.gov.ie/eng/News/Taoiseach%27s_Speeches/Speech_by_the_Taoiseach_Mr_Leo_Varadkar_TD_Queen_s_University_Friday_4_August_2017_-_The_Future_of_Relationships_North_and_South_.html.

"Verhofstadt says a hard border would be a 'disaster'", *RTE News*, 20 September, available at: https://www.rte.ie/news/2017/0920/906100-brexit/.

Villiers, T. (2016a) "Democracy was the reason I had to back Leave campaign", *The Guardian*, 25 June, available at: https://www.theguardian.com/commentisfree/2016/jun/25/theresa-villiers-democracy-was-the-reason-i-backed-brexit.

Villiers, T. (2016b) "Vote Leave, and take back control", Speech to the *Financial Times* Future of Europe conference, 14 April, available at: https://www.theresavilliers.co.uk/news/vote-leave-and-take-back-control-speech-theresa-villiers.

Watts, D. & C. Pilkington (2005) *Britain in the European Union Today* (3rd edition), Manchester, Manchester University Press.

Welsh Government (2017) "Securing Wales' future: Transition from the European Union to a new relationship with Europe", Cardiff: Welsh Government, available at: https://beta.gov.wales/sites/default/files/2017-01/30683%20Securing%20Wales%C2%B9%20Future_ENGLISH_WEB.pdf.

Wilson, R. (2016) "Northern Ireland peace monitoring report", No. 4, September, Belfast: Community Relations Council, available at: https://www.community-relations.org.uk/sites/crc/files/media-files/NIPMR-Final-2016.pdf.

Zürn, M. (2016) "Opening up Europe: Next steps in politicisation research", *West European Politics* 39 (1): 164–82.

Index